BACK IN CONTROL

First Sentient Publications edition, 2004

Cover design by Kim Johansen, Black Dog Design
Book design by Nicholas Cummings and Rudy Ramos

Library of Congress Cataloging-in-Publication Data

Wilson, Diane Grimard, [date]
  Back in control : how to stay sane, productive, and inspired in
your career transition / Diane Grimard Wilson.-- 1st Sentient
Publications ed.
      p. cm.
  Includes index.
  ISBN 1-59181-016-7
  1. Career changes. 2. Career changes--Psychological aspects. 3.
Self-control. 4. Career development. I. Title.
HF5384.W545 2004
650.1--dc22

                                      2004003957

Printed in the United States of America

10 9 8 7 6 5 4 3 2 1

SENTIENT PUBLICATIONS

A Limited Liability Company
1113 Spruce St.
Boulder, CO 80302
www.sentientpublications.com

BACK IN CONTROL

HOW TO STAY SANE, PRODUCTIVE, AND INSPIRED IN YOUR CAREER TRANSITION

Diane Grimard Wilson

SENTIENT PUBLICATIONS, LLC

CONTENTS

INTRODUCTION

My father worked forty-two years on his first job. If my mother hears me say this, she carefully adds that when he left his job, he *retired*—he wasn't *fired* (which is almost a profanity to her). My mother "didn't work" when I was young; instead she stayed at home to take care of her eight children. My father labored hard to support the family. The question of whether he loved his work was as irrelevant as whether it expressed his soul or inner being. He was a loyal worker who used his skill and dedication to provide well for our family.

In the evenings when I would tiptoe into the basement, I could see my father back in a corner at his workbench, surrounded by radios, televisions, and other electrical gadgets in various stages of disrepair. Incredibly resourceful, he had taught himself electronics and would fix things when they broke. My father seemed to love any electrical device he could take apart to make better. Even as a small child, I got the impression that once something was broken, the parts didn't all go back together as easily as they came apart. Nonetheless, sitting and patiently puzzling things out was his passion.

Work and life has changed in the last forty years. From the outside, my own career seems to sharply contrast with that of my parents. I am a married woman who works full time outside my home. I own a small company in a very big city. I have no children and spend many of my waking moments thinking about what type of work people should do next, and how they can secure it and do it better. Yet, on the inside, my parents' values of honesty, dedication, and loyalty are at the core of my very being. For this, I am most grateful.

In the early 1980's when I titled my master's thesis in psychology, I used the term "career choices" instead of "vocational choices."

However, career was a rather new concept then. I knew little of what the future would bring in terms of career changes, the shift in perception of what work means to people, and the downsizing, merging, and other unheard-of strategies that dominate organizational activities today. Organizations not only announce layoffs when things are economically tough, they also use layoffs to manage their budgets when things are going well. Further, research shows that we can all expect to make between five and seven changes in our own careers.

Sigmund Freud said that mentally healthy people need to be able to do two things: to love and to work. Most people trained in psychology have focused on the love side—relationships. My focus has always been on work: what people do at work, how they choose it, and most importantly, how they manage change. In almost twenty years in the field, I have been involved in executive coaching, team building, and broader organizational development projects, but a large portion of my time has been focused on coaching individuals on career transition issues.

So, day in and day out, you are most likely to find me in my office sitting in a comfortable, rounded, dark-blue chair across from one just like it, listening to and talking with a client. My clients are my focus; their issues are my fascination. I can hardly believe anyone would call what I do work, as I feel privileged to do it. I hear my clients' stories and dilemmas and act as their sounding board, resource, and guide as we try to puzzle things out. As my father's daughter, the last part is my personal passion. I feel lucky to be able to make a living at it.

WHY THIS BOOK NOW?

Over the years, one of my most poignant observations about coaching people in career change has been how confusing and isolating transition can be. Whether the change is voluntary ("I quit!") or imposed from the outside ("You're fired!"), most people feel lost and alone at some point. This can negatively impact their progress, their life, and the people closest to them.

This sense of feeling lost is not surprising. Many of my clients have parents with work histories like those of my mother and father. We Baby Boomers, like subsequent generations, have received little psychological preparation for today's almost cyclic challenges of finding work, confronting transition, and reinventing ourselves to be more marketable.

I often think that if only my clients could get a clearer understanding of the learning process and mindset needed to navigate change, they would be able to move through it easier, faster, and better. Transition would be more of an opportunity than a chore. Their darker days would get lighter faster. They would be able to anchor themselves in their own lives much more deeply, and make more authentic commitments to future work.

In my years of listening to my clients' stories of struggles and courage, I have often wished these individuals could hear each other. Perhaps it would be like some double-screened Woody Allen movie: my 3:00 Wednesday appointment—an information systems guy—could hear my 4:00 marketing manager discuss how joining a professional association really was a good idea and how adding physical exercise to his day lifted his mood incredibly. After listening to each other's insights, each would feel less alone and much more appreciated and validated in his current life and his search for a better career situation. Unfortunately, those who seem most isolated are the ones least likely to join a group of kindred spirits. They often, however, like to read. If you fit this description, then this book is especially for you.

OVERVIEW: AN UNUSUAL CAREER BOOK

This book is a companion for you when your life is undergoing change, particularly career change. This includes when you:

- have quit your job or have been fired or laid off
- would like to quit, make a change, or even be laid off
- are entering or re-entering the world of work

It's an unusual book because it is not designed to help you with the typical career-change challenges such as managing the résumé, researching the Internet, and interviewing. Instead, it will help you manage something perhaps more difficult—yourself. So, if you have ever felt stuck, depressed, dejected, lazy, that you have no skills or future, or that you couldn't concentrate on what's needed to make a change anyway, this book is for you. For many of us, self-management in transition is no small task. For most, it is the most important.

In this book, I will be speaking to you as a coach and counselor. I will share my expertise and compassion as well as the experiences that have been part of my clients' many successful career journeys. My expertise comes from years of operating my own career counseling and coaching practice. The compassion comes from my own humbling transitions and the privilege of sitting across from countless people caught in the psychological free fall that often accompanies career change.

These experiences have taught me that it is possible to manage the mental and emotional underpinnings of transition to your benefit. Wisdom, wholeness, and strength can come from well-handled transitions—as messy as they can be. In fact, your life can become even better than it was before you started. In the ten chapters that follow, I will describe and illustrate key lessons to help you navigate your change. These lessons can lead to a new way of looking at your transition and offer many action tips to increase your emotional balance, confidence, intuition, energy, and productivity. You'll learn more about who you are and how to get where you really want to go.

This book not only provides you with a coach to educate and inspire you, it also offers a bit of community. The lessons are illustrated wherever possible by the voices of others in career transition journeys and stories based on composite characters I created from the lives of clients, colleagues, and friends. You will hear their real-life experiences in rich and candid detail—this is the stuff that we want to ask others about but are seldom in a position to. Chock full of practical ideas, the text is intimate, sometimes humorous, and always reassuring. Reading it will help you to stay on your path and will enrich your life and work.

Road Map of the Book

This book is organized around my belief that career transition is best viewed as a learning process. We can all suffer from ill-fitting beliefs and expectations about what transition is like, how we should feel in it, how to find a job—especially one we feel passionate about—and even who we really are. With this learning attitude, you can become much smarter about who you are, what you need, what you can do, and what your best strategics are.

The Chapters

Each chapter presents a lesson pivotal to managing yourself in career change. Chapters one through three help you understand the terrain of transition, create a context for your own transition story, and identify demons and potholes you might find along the way. Chapters four through nine give you a set of resources and rituals to keep you on track. You will see how your behavioral style, thoughts, feelings, intuition, friends, and even Feng Shui can help you make progress. Chapter ten provides insights and advice from myself and others to inspire you to look forward and make the most of the transition.

You can pick the chapters that most appeal to you to read first, but it's best to read the complete text and then go back and focus on key areas. All the chapters end with writing exercises to strengthen your insights through personal reflection. Chapters five through nine also have action-oriented assignments to apply directly to your transition.

How This Book Can Help You

This book will coach you through a number of important aspects of making successful career and life changes. It will help you to:

- cultivate inspiration and hope
- become smarter about change and transition

- see your own barriers and learn how to deal with them
- understand your behavioral style and how to use it to your advantage
- condition your mind for success
- handle your emotions more effectively
- cultivate intuition and hear your "little voice" better
- structure your environment to enhance your focus and productivity
- help others to be useful to you instead of adding to your stress
- learn the lessons you were meant to learn in transition

I hope my book will be a valuable companion as you confront career changes—either voluntary or involuntary ones. I intend it to be a book that you will read and reread and feel stronger from reminding yourself that you can take control and make a difference in your own life, even when that seems hard. I'd like this book to encourage you that things are going to be okay, you can be better for having been down this road, you're not alone, and there are many things that will help.

Starting this project became my own journey. At points, the evolution of this book touched my life in some very personal and powerful ways and I was not always the objective expert I first intended to be, commenting from the outside. Instead, I was a participant with my own stories, and I've included some of them in the book when I think they might help you.

CHAPTER ONE

GET SMART ABOUT
WHAT'S HAPPENING

*Looking back, I wish I could have gotten it into my head that there were
things that I didn't know. I didn't know what I really wanted, how I might
feel after being laid off, or even the best way to find meaningful work. I
actually had no idea of what I was doing for a long time.*

Glen, fifty-two, laid off from his position as an electronic engineer
for a large telecommunications company five months ago, salary
$70,000

A change in career is something nearly everyone experiences.
You get laid off or fired, find yourself in a situation that no
longer fits for you, start yearning for more meaningful work, or
decide to return to a full-time job after a leave. At these junctures,
many of us react in one of the following ways. We may:

- pounce into action blinded by a need to take control
- bury our heads in the sand and try to ignore it
- get stuck in a wide-eyed, "deer in the headlights" panic

This chapter provides you with another response: get smart
about what is happening. That means understanding the inner
workings of your career transition so you can make the most effective decisions. Certainly, in an immediate crisis you may need to
react without reflection. This chapter begins after that reaction. It
requires that you simultaneously challenge and expand your knowledge and beliefs. It also gives you a powerful way of thinking that

will transform your experiences—however difficult they are—into wisdom for your career and life.

Even Smart People Can Learn Better Moves

Many people have misconceptions about career change. They have preconceived notions about how they *should* feel, but no real idea of the hidden psychological challenges they face. They do not even know how best to search for a job. Across occupations and job levels, misconceptions are held by all kinds of people, including those who have been very successful in their careers. Often the most successful people can have the most difficulty with handling transitions they consider failures—such as being fired. If it's never happened to you, you might not understand how to recover.

Further, most of us don't know what we don't know. Therefore, you can spend a lot of time doing things that don't produce results and conclude that you just need to try harder. One example would be the lackluster salesperson. Her personality is completely out of sync with her career goal. Yet she just keeps trying, convinced her new position may be just around the next corner. Another would be the executive who puts a heavy emphasis on using the Internet to find a job. The probability of success through simply responding to job postings on the Internet is extremely low, especially for a senior executive. But he doesn't know this.

When you're searching for a job, it is highly unlikely that someone (other than your coach, if you have one) will notice where you are going wrong and tell you. I have seen people spend hours and days on very ill-conceived strategies, believing their frustration is a necessary part of the process. It's not. Unchecked, these actions will make the emotional experience of unemployment more trying than it needs to be. Inevitably, part of the work of transition must be about refining or even changing what we believe is true about ourselves and the world around us. In this book, I will help you do this. As we work together, you'll have the opportunity to make your career as well as your life even better than they were before.

EMOTIONAL EMPLOYMENT AND EMOTIONAL UNEMPLOYMENT

Emotional employment and *emotional unemployment* are key terms for understanding the messages of this book. Here's how I came up with them.

Emotional Employment: Watching Oprah at Work

Have you ever watched Oprah at work? Tune into her show and you can see her attentively interviewing people, asking important and hard questions. Curious, candid and compassionate. She looks like nothing in the world is more important or fun, and that her job allows her to share herself in a most authentic way. If you are like most people, being able to use your whole self and best skills at work is tremendously motivating. *Emotional employment* describes this important dimension of your relationship to work.

I believe the commitments we make or hope to make at work can be as important as the ones we make in our relationships. People say, "At the end of my life I certainly won't be wishing I had worked more." Yet, in reality, many people do place their work commitment right on par with their love relationships. They feel a sense of purpose and deep satisfaction by contributing their talents. For example, a mother who loves her new baby immensely may also experience a longing to go back to her job and use other parts of herself. Many men and women enjoy and look forward to their vacations but feel a sense of relief when they return to work they enjoy. Our work commitments can ground us.

Emotional Unemployment: Ungrounded Territory

When we are not absorbed in meaningful work, we can feel tremendously ungrounded. I call this ungrounded psychological territory *emotional unemployment*. You can be emotionally unemployed after you have been let go, fired, laid off, or even while working in a position that isn't right for you.

Emotional unemployment is becoming more prevalent and difficult since companies are firing and laying off more people than ever before. Also, it can be very difficult to find a job to commit to during tough economic times. There are degrees of emotional unemployment. On some jobs you can feel very emotionally employed and on others relatively unemployed, no matter how much you are paid. Also, between jobs, some people connect so much with unpaid work experiences that they don't suffer the same emotional unemployment dissatisfaction and disorientation that others experience without paid work.

I believe that work develops like a love commitment when we have the opportunity to use certain parts of ourselves. The more you get to experience the sides of yourself you value, the more committed you are likely to become. For example, I love being a coach and writer. In both of these roles, I feel like myself in some crucial ways. I feel whole after I write; it's like the best part of me gets to be free. Not only do I like some of the recognition from family and friends that comes with being a writer, but more importantly, I love the act of writing and making meaning. We can easily become committed to situations that meet our needs and allow us to be most fully alive.

A career transition can be a learning process. The following chapters will help you structure a journey to manage yourself as well as learn more about who you are. Increased self-knowledge can allow you to create a work situation where you can more easily have the deep satisfaction of emotional employment. But first, you need to know that there are real and important practical steps to finding a job, and you need to examine what these are.

Four Truths About Career Change

To help you get smart about what's happening, this chapter presents four basic truths about career change. Understanding any one of these truths could make a huge, potentially life-changing difference to you. These truths will also help you understand the chapters that follow.

The four truths are:

- Most people who experience career losses feel like you do.
- There will be predictable stages in your career transition.

- As an adult, you will continue to grow and change.
- There really *is* a best way to approach finding a new job.

Exploring these four truths will help you create more realistic expectations. In doing so, you'll be less likely to slide into paralyzing isolation, frustration, or depression, and more likely to capitalize on the tremendous opportunities for creating a satisfying career and life.

Truth One: Most People Feel Just Like You Do

> I was called into the office in the afternoon on Friday. I thought I was going to get a raise after all my work on the last project. I should have known something was up when I saw the HR manager sitting there with my boss. He was nervous as he told me my job was being eliminated. I was stunned and after a moment, started to cry. I couldn't stop myself.
>
> Colleen, forty, former division manager of a multinational consulting firm, two months after leaving her company, salary $90,000

When you confront a major loss such as being laid off or fired, you may experience a predictable sequence of feelings. Some of the stages of grieving Dr. Elizabeth Kubler-Ross identified—such as denial, bargaining, anger, despair, and acceptance—have relevance for career losses. Understanding this sequence can help you create distance and cultivate compassion for your emotions, but often it's not the whole picture. The second part of this section will give you additional ideas for understanding your emotional world after career loss.

Denial Stage

First is denial. I'm sure we all have been in situations involving a loss. For a while you may feel like you're okay and have your wits about you, and in some ways you do. But the event of change can seem unbelievable. You may think: *This can't be happening to me. This didn't really happen.* Or, *It's no big deal.*

Here are a couple of examples of people experiencing denial. I have worked with outplacement groups who spent whole days training together on writing résumés, interviewing, and networking because their company was closing. In conversations, these people often talked about the company and their role in it as if they were going to return the next day. They would even start planning the office holiday party. The only thing was, they weren't going back. One kind, quiet, steady, middle-aged administrative services manager told his group that he had been getting up every morning at the same time he did when he was working. He'd start to put on his work clothes and get ready and then realize the plant had closed. As he spoke, everyone nodded with a sympathetic smile. He probably wasn't the only one doing this.

The more traumatic the job loss, the more denial you can experience. You may only be able to let yourself grapple with the reality of the loss in small doses. I remember one interview that sports icon Michael Jordan gave after his father's murder. Rather than secluding himself in his grief, he resumed playing golf. When the interviewer asked him how he was dealing with this terrible loss, he paused and said: "A little at a time." Denial, whether conscious or unconscious, provides us with a shelter until we can gradually face the reality of what has happened, along with its potential consequences. It is easy to misjudge ourselves and others if we don't understand what denial is.

Bargaining Stage

After this protective shock wears off, many of us move into bargaining. This stage is often a natural part of job layoff situations when there is uncertainty about who will stay, who will go, when they'll leave, and why. In bargaining, your thought strategies will feature "if, then" elements: *If I do a good job on this project, then maybe I'll be the one who gets to stay.* Your thinking may also reflect a childlike logic: *If I make it through this red light, my plant will stay open at least six more months.*

The preoccupation with trying to control things over which we have no control, or finding justice where there is none, is like mental gum chewing. It keeps our minds busy and somewhat content. It's easier for us to continue to focus on what *should* happen than to confront our feelings about what *is* happening to us. It gives us a sense of power to try to understand it all. Bargaining can serve the function of comforting us until we can do better.

Like all defensive reactions, bargaining becomes a problem when it becomes extreme. We've all seen people who get obsessed with what is happening even though they have no control over the outcome. This type of preoccupation can keep us from listening to ourselves, facing the situation, and taking charge of what we *can* control. And, in the end, the only things we really can control are what we are learning and how we are moving ahead.

Anger Stage

It's all their fault . . . I hate those people . . . They ruined my life. These sentiments are typical of the anger stage. Here, your feelings can range from general irritability to rage. One client told me about waking up and feeling, for no rational reason at all, like every cell of his body was filled with rage. The rest of the day he was cross with his family, curt with others outside his home, and generally tense and ill-tempered.

It's true that life or careers can provide ample justification for anger. However, a part of us does not *like* change. During a major disruption like the loss of a job, a pervasive sense of anger can just be part of the territory. If you can understand this, you'll be better at stepping outside your emotions and knowing you don't have to ferret out another reason for your anger if there really isn't one. And knowing that you don't have to act on your anger may save you from some costly consequences.

Anger is tricky for many of us. I have worked with a number of clients, especially males, who believed they weren't angry when their actions revealed something different. One outplacement training group had a very angry man named Kip. He was a longtime employee in a plant whose closing had been handled very poorly. Kip tapped his pencil expectantly, frowned, and was aloof most of the session. However, as he pointedly announced during the Kubler-Ross discussion, he was "not *angry!*"

Then, in a practice employment interview role-play, Kip was my applicant. As our interview progressed, I asked him how he felt about his plant closing. Without hesitation, he flew into a diatribe featuring a very candid and detailed account of how he had been wronged. He ranted on and on. Finally he stopped, shook his head and said: "I can't believe I just did that!" Stunned, he then relaxed, softened, and said, "I guess I *am* angry!" He had every right to be so, and accepting his feelings allowed him to start moving past them.

Depression Stage

When we blame others, we tend to become angry. When we blame ourselves, we tend to become depressed. Blaming ourselves is the hallmark of the next stage—depression. It's natural to experience some level of depression when dealing with change, especially a change you didn't expect or want. In this stage, some of the pain comes from what we tell ourselves and what we believe.

People can develop irrational beliefs when depressed. For example, a client once told me:

> Even though I'm just a lowly quality tech, I can close a manu-facturing plant! You see, on my first job out of school, I was there for one year and the plant abruptly closed. My second job lasted two years and again the plant closed. I moved here from Omaha and tried to make a fresh start in Chicago. Now it's nine months and this plant is going belly up too.

He initially laughed about it. But after a while, this belief about his work life became more and more evident and revealed a deep sense of powerlessness. Getting my client to examine and change that belief wasn't easy, especially in a difficult economy.

Depression can not only make you feel powerless, it can engage your self-critic and challenge your self-esteem. Here are some examples: *You should have seen this coming. If only you had majored in architecture and not business. If only you had kept your mouth shut with your boss at the holiday party.* Other people may feel that nothing they could have done in the past, or can now do in the present, would make a difference.

Some degree of anger and depression is a natural part of confronting loss. However, if you are incapacitated by sadness or a sense of futility, have trouble sleeping, are eating too much or too little, or are feeling self-destructive, consult a professional for additional help. With the right support, you can work through these feelings to make your life richer, stronger, and better.

Acceptance Stage

If we allow ourselves to move through the stages above, we come to acceptance. As though the sun is finally peeking through the clouds, we see life more clearly and realistically. We stop finding fault with ourselves, because we know that it wasn't completely our fault no matter what the situation was. We also know it's a waste of our valuable energy to keep blaming others. We can tell ourselves *What's done is done,* and while we may not like it, we accept it. At this point, our energies become free from the emotional demands of the earlier stages. We are finally able to put things behind us and commit to a new path.

Is This Sequence the Whole Picture?

The one-word answer to that question is: no. After a loss, you may neatly progress through this sequence of stages or you may not. Most probably, you will not. That doesn't mean there is anything wrong with you. Some people start with acceptance and move backwards. Others experience this whole cycle, in one direction or the other, several times within a period of days or even an hour. For example, if you've lost your job and get an interview with a desirable firm, you may suddenly leap to acceptance: *Yes, it happened, and though I was angry at my company for a long time, I'm now putting this behind me and starting anew. Ah yes, life is good.*

If the interview doesn't work out, you may again feel angry and depressed: *Not again! Oh, this just makes me hate those guys at my old company even more. Their stupid strategic plan—any moron would have known it would have driven us into the ground. But what was I thinking? Nothing good ever happens to me anyway.* If you can see what is going on inside you and understand it, you'll have more control over it.

This is how some others have described their experiences in transition:

> My feelings range all across the board on a typical day. Often in the morning, I'm bummed when I get up and have no place to go. Then, once I do get going, I feel much better. On days that I feel like I've made some progress, I feel pretty good. Also, I feel that I need to socialize. I often make plans for the evening. I work at trying to maintain a good attitude.
>
> Nancy, late thirties, formerly director of marketing in health care, after searching for a job for a month

> My feelings and attitudes go from soup to nuts on any given day. I begin with a positive attitude, but when I'm not actively engaged in work or social activities, my mind sways to the negative side, and I feel the frustration of not having a fulfilling job.
>
> Madelyn, thirty-two, formerly a customer service representative at a payroll firm, attempting to find work after being fired three months earlier

> I feel like it's a constant battle between hope and discouragement. My tendency toward extremes is most apparent when I'm in a transition. So, I'll awake either hopeful for the day and the opportunities and successes it might bring, or discouraged and depressed, consciously making the effort to get up and get to the first phone call or web search. Then, so quickly, based on a good lead or one that goes nowhere, a promising phone call, or one with a negative person, I'll be so quickly at the other end of this spectrum. Winning the battle means success, means balance, perspective, pressing on,

realizing that I, me, my whole self, continues to exist outside the realm of this career transition.

Jennifer, twenty-five, completed graduate school two months before

While it may not be possible to predict the feelings you will have on any given day, your knowledge of the Kubler-Ross stages can prepare you for the range of feelings you may have. Feelings that, as you can see from above, can also be greatly influenced by the immediate circumstances.

Throughout the rest of this book, especially in chapter six, "Let Your Emotions Be Your Strength," you'll learn strategies to help you better manage the emotional side of career change. For now, you are about to learn about the three stages within a career transition, which may be far more predictable than your emotional responses to them.

Truth Two: There Will Be Stages to Your Career Transition

In working with my clients, I have found the writings of William Bridges quite valuable. His book, *Transitions* (1980), has helped many create a basic road map for navigating their career transitions. Here is a summary of some of his key points.

First, transition is the personal experience of integrating external change into your sense of who you are. External events may include getting fired, laid off, or even taking a new job. Transition takes place as you reorganize yourself to adapt to the change.

Secondly, transition is composed of three phases: Endings, the Neutral Zone, and Beginnings. Overall, these three phases encompass a sequence of orientation, disorientation, and reorientation—all considered part of the natural process of personal development and transformation.

Your knowledge of these stages can help you decode what you are experiencing, spend your time productively, and stop feeling like you are crazy when you're not. Let's take a close look at each.

Stage One: Endings

At first blush, "endings" doesn't seem like the most logical place to start this three-stage process. However, to begin a new path, we must leave the old one behind. When I talk about endings, I am referring to the internal experience of leaving rather than the external experience. In some cases, the internal experience of saying goodbye to your job may have occurred before you even left the company. We have all met people who go to work every day but left their jobs emotionally years ago. In other cases, internal endings can occur long after you have physically left your job.

I have worked with a number of people whose central task in finding a new job was to reach closure on their previous one. Bridges writes that it is only through emptying out and creating a void that we can allow something else to come to our attention. This is why many people have to physically leave a job before they can find a new one. They have to unwind for a while before they have energy to consider new options.

Many people find saying goodbye to the person they were in their last job a daunting task. As one client said, "Diane, how can I do something different? I am a banker and will always be a banker." And he will stay right there, unless he can let that image of himself go, at least a little.

From working with both groups and individuals undergoing change, I have found that the endings stage may be complex and fluid rather than cut and dried. It may not be easy to just say goodbye to the sense of who you are in certain job roles. Sometimes you also need to start planning and implementing the next steps, even if you haven't emotionally finished what you were doing. It is important to recognize that you must ultimately put closure on a job that has ended. However, all-or-nothing thinking on any front can stymie your progress in career change.

Stage Two: The Neutral Zone

> Throughout my life I have always had goals that I was work-
> ing toward. Right now, I have no idea of who I am or what I
> want. And most of the time, I don't really care.
>
> Lauren, fifty-one, psychologist, laid off from her position in senior
> care four months earlier

> Having worked for my last company for over thirty years, I
> don't think I'll have any idea of what I really want to do for
> about a year. I'm taking a working sabbatical—helping my
> wife in her business and doing some volunteer environmental
> work. I'll make more decisions after I get my bearings.
>
> Will, fifty-six, purchasing agent who left an ailing company for an
> early retirement five months ago

Having said goodbye to what was, we enter what Bridges calls
the Neutral Zone. Most people who contact me for career coaching
are in the Neutral Zone. Their next step is not yet in view, but their
attachment to what was has diminished or is gone. The Neutral
Zone can be a confusing and frightening stage. In fact, you can feel
like you are falling apart. This feeling makes sense if we subscribe to
Bridges's view that our whole way of being is held within a given life
pattern of bonds, relationships, and roles. Take away the roles we
play and the relationships we have in the workplace and that pattern falls to pieces. I see someone in this stage as a puzzle that's been
broken apart. Your goal is to find a new order, pattern, and vision to
organize the pieces.

The Neutral Zone can be a creative time, if you can understand
and experience it as such. Without this understanding, it will probably be quite challenging. It is a time for taking stock, for soul
searching, and for figuring out what is important. This is an opportunity for deeper self-definition that cannot happen when you continue to see yourself in terms of the roles you played in your job and
the relationships and habits you had there. When you empty yourself

of those old self-images, you can consider who you really are today and who you want to become.

It is powerful to watch people transform. People become whole and learn to shape their lives when they connect to something larger than themselves. This applies to people who consider themselves religious as well as those who do not. The larger thing could be nature, a group, family, or spirituality. Most of us who observe such transformations could never deny the pivotal role of spirituality. Many people find their true passion, purpose, or calling by first strengthening their connection with a higher power they call God.

Overall, the Neutral Zone is mystical, frightening, and rich with potential for growth. You will see the phenomenal quality of this phase in many of the chapters that follow. Reading about the experiences of others can enhance your courage and inspiration for moving through your own Neutral Zone.

Stage Three: Beginnings

Bridges refers to the final stage of a transition as Beginnings. This, of course, is contrary to popular wisdom that a beginning would be the starting point. If you have done the work of the two earlier stages, you'll be stronger for your struggles and bring in a new wisdom from the journey. You will be able to begin another phase of your life with sincerity, commitment, and the energy of your new way of being. But rest assured, transition is cyclic. Before long, you will confront another external change and move again into Endings, only to begin the whole sequence again.

The Promise of Working Through These Stages

Having worked with many, many people in the middle of the career-change hurricane, I can testify that personal transition can be difficult. But resisting transition is usually even more difficult. As Bridges says, your energy will be tied up in trying to perpetuate what was, or in avoiding the not-knowing stage of what will be. No one wants to confront the emptiness we must allow ourselves to experience to create the new. And that makes it hard to visualize and create—much less commit to—what we want next.

If you embrace transition in the best way you can, at your own pace, you will allow a renewal of yourself and your life that can exceed your previous dreams. Even in the most unfair, difficult, and unworkable situations, you can become a stronger, happier, more effective, and more loving person. I've seen it happen again and again.

Our culture puts a strong emphasis on the accumulation of material possessions. Other cultures value the accumulation of personal wisdom more highly. When you begin to see transition as an opportunity to develop a more profound wisdom, an important shift in your thinking can occur. This shift can allow you to get unstuck and move more freely through your Neutral Zone. In the following section, you will discover another truth to help you get and stay unstuck.

Truth Three: Even Adults Continue to Grow and Change

We all have some idea of the stages that children go through in their development, like the terrible twos and first words, steps, and teeth. Most of us, however, have no idea that as adults we also go through developmental stages, many of which are positive. Usually, the only changes we consider possible for adults, aside from the dreaded aging of our bodies, involve negative stereotypes, such as the mid-life crisis or the seven-year itch.

As a result of our society's negative preconceptions about aging, many of us didn't look ahead. When my generation, the Baby Boomers, was coming of age, one bit of popular wisdom was "don't trust anyone over thirty." It wasn't until we neared age thirty that the other side of that marker had any interest. Decades ago, no one could have imagined that Mick Jagger and the Rolling Stones would still be performing well into their fifties or that we would find that exciting. Even Mick was once quoted as saying he couldn't imagine still performing at age thirty. Our understanding of age was an us/them equation with "us" being young and "them" being old.

When we got to be the age of "them," we embraced another piece of popular wisdom. "If you work hard, then you can retire and relax." Now with longer life expectancies and advances in health care, we all plan to live longer and better. However, most of the people I see who are in their fifties do not find the thought of relaxing in a hammock all day appealing, nor do they wish to continue doing what they are currently doing forever. Words like retirement have come to feel less relevant for many as they grow older.

The truth is, we do keep growing as adults. Our interests and values shift with age, time, and life experiences. I've noticed that many people experience a fundamental shift in who they are and what they want about every seven to ten years. Because we have not been prepared to expect these changes, they can be disconcerting and alarming. But take comfort! If a career that fit at one point in your life does not fit now, you are not alone.

Sometimes I talk with people who are experiencing these shifts and have no confidence in their ability to make career decisions. They hear a resounding chorus in their heads that reflects their misconceptions and may sound like this:

If only I'd majored in my first choice at school, I wouldn't be in this predicament right now.

My response: Potentially untrue—you may have liked that major and the career that went with it for a while and still have needed a change by now.

I must be stupid, since I'm fifty-one years old and have no idea what I want to do.

My advice: Stop being hard on yourself. You may not be ready to make a decision, since you are undergoing a personal reconstruction that is normal at this juncture in your life.

Everyone else seems to know what they want.

I believe that everyone has a unique developmental path to follow.

During a shift, there may be a period of time in which you have no idea of what you'd like to do. It happens to many! The reason is that as you grow, you end the earlier versions of yourself that you are leaving behind. This state of not knowing is part of the Neutral

Zone in which you are reconstructing. Therefore, cultivating a vision of who you are is very important. This will be the focus of chapter two, "Know Your Own Story." But before you embark on that chapter, you need to understand more about finding a new job or career.

Truth Four: There Really Is a Best Way to Find a New Job

Before you go further into the inner work of your transition, you must be smart about the practical, external side of the job search. Being certain you've chosen the best way to approach your search— and there *is* a best way—will certainly diminish your emotional distress.

There are hundreds of excellent technical books on the practical aspects of the job search. I've included a list of my favorites in the Resource appendix. It is not the intention of this book to replace any of them—instead, it should be a valuable companion to the job search manual of your choice. Nevertheless, I will now distill for you the basics of what you need to do for the practical side of the job search. These are basics that most, if not all, of the technical books on the market will offer.

- **Know What You Offer.** Take stock. Discover and take inventory of your skills, passions, assets, and options for career choices. There are tests and written exercises to help increase your clarity. The outcome of these efforts is a profile that reflects an assessment of who you are and what you bring to the work situation. So many people target careers that don't suit them or try to write a résumé before knowing their assets. Doing a good self-assessment is important and will save you time.

- **Know Where You Want to Work.** Ask yourself: Where can I best use my talents? Where will I be happiest? What is the best fit? Informational interviewing is important at this stage to get an inside look at what you think you want to do and where. Certain trade-offs are always involved when you take a new position. However, your research will allow you to understand the potential cost of what you are trading off, and to identify what you really need.

- **Know What Potential Employers Will Be Looking For.** Identify the concerns of organizations where you do want to work. What do they need? What would help them? What matters most is what you can do for them. Do you see how different this is from just randomly sending out a résumé? That is an extremely weak job search strategy, almost guaranteed to bring poor results and distress.

- **Know How to Sell Yourself.** You will best promote yourself by showing that you can meet the needs of your target employers. This step is where you think about your résumé and other marketing tools such as the interview. Most people start with the résumé too early and then get stuck, because they don't know what to say or how to say it. If you've done research on yourself and your targets, it's easier to be confident in selling yourself. You'll know what you're doing!

- **Refine What You Know.** Continue to collect information. Figure out the best ways to contact the people who may need you and who will make hiring decisions. Examine what is and is not working so that you won't get stuck in useless job search strategies or applying for positions that aren't right for you anyway. Practice presenting yourself. Keep at it and don't get stuck in your emotional reactions. If you do, learn from it.

The most challenging part of confronting changes in your career is that typically you don't know what you don't know. That's why this book starts with the message that you need to focus on getting smart about what's happening. This chapter explored four essential truths about career changes. Knowing any one of these can save you a great deal of time and frustration. It can also help you avoid emotional unemployment—the distress of not having a commitment to work that has meaning or purpose.

If you're like many people who have tried the practical steps for finding a job recommended by the career manuals and still haven't made the progress you had hoped for, read on. Or, if you got stuck before you could even do one of these steps, still read on. Like the inner game of golf, my premise is that the mental and emotional underpinnings of your career change are the most important. Addressing these can help you feel back in control and create the work and life you deserve.

This framework can help you separate out your unproductive efforts from your effective ones when emotional unemployment becomes taxing. The biggest mistake people make at this point is failing to take the time to understand themselves. Everyone would rather skip these self-assessment tasks and spring into their preconceived notions of what they consider to be the best action. The following chapter, "Know Your Own Story," goes beyond self-assessment and asks you to consider an even bigger question: What does this change mean to you? What *can* it mean to you? Knowing your own story can give you a larger picture of yourself and help move you from being mired in procrastination or resistance to actively creating your own legacy. It's time to become your own hero by knowing your story.

WRITING REFLECTION EXERCISES

1. How would you describe your predominant emotional reactions in your career transition? Give examples:

2. What phase of Bridges's model best describes your career transition today? Explain.

3. Is emotional employment a strong motivator for you?

4. What are your key personal insights from this chapter?

5. What are the next steps you will take as a result of this chapter?

6. In what other ways can you apply this chapter?

CHAPTER TWO

KNOW YOUR OWN STORY

I was unhappy in my job and not comfortable with the people I worked with. Without warning or notice, I was told I was being let go. Three weeks later, I worked my last day. It took me several weeks to regroup as I was unsure whether I wanted to stay in marketing or change fields. The dismissal made me question my abilities. Added to that, I was dealing with a lot of self-induced anxiety and some depression that further exacerbated the situation.

Jeff, early forties, formerly director of marketing for mid-sized firm, salary $60,000

If you're like a lot of my clients, you may experience a range of feelings during your transition. For this reason, when I started to dream of writing this book, I was certain I wanted to include the voices of real people. I wanted these voices to speak to you as I heard them and to provide you with a community of fellow travelers. I hoped they would be able to tell you the things most friends or even family members don't tell each other, things that need to be talked about and understood. It is a sure sign that a client is beginning to trust me when she finally asks: "Diane, do other people ever go through this?" That's what's isolating—thinking you are alone in your journey. You're not.

Chapter two is designed to help you get past that sense of isolation and to increase your clarity about your own transition. It reflects a basic premise of the book that understanding what you are going through makes it easier for you to stay sane, productive, and inspired during times of change. Good information can help you cultivate the sense of control and perspective that everyone needs to make progress.

COLLECTING VOICES

To collect voices for this book, I conducted a number of workshops over a period of sixteen months. In small groups, I asked the participants hard questions about their career transitions. They wrote and then read their responses aloud. The experience proved to be powerful, but in a way I did not initially expect.

Each session began with a writing exercise to help participants introduce themselves as well as to leave the events of their day outside the group room. The exercise was to describe their career transition—when and how it started and what it meant to them. They were asked to tell the story with themselves as the hero. The exercise was designed to move them into answering the harder questions of their transitions and exploring their emotions and their progress.

A number of the groups included people I had known for a long time. I knew some of their stories as well as they did. But often writing and reading them out loud seemed to change things. In some cases there was a shift I could actually see. It was as though these difficult feelings became more resolved; the painful events were more behind them. Psychologically complex experiences became a little simpler and more manageable—they were stories. My participants, as writers, were the heroes.

YOUR STORY

Writing your story—even if it's only a partial version of it—can give you power to transform it. The process of describing your situation in writing forces you to take the perspective of the storyteller. It can reorganize your relationship to the information, provide a certain distance, and put this moment of your misery, joy, and uncertainty into a larger context. It makes it clear that this moment is not your destiny, even if it seems like it. Further, it can allow you to begin to accept your past a little better, even if you don't like what happened to you. In doing so, you can begin to reclaim the energy that's consumed by wishing it wasn't true.

So, knowing your own story can mean being able to step outside of it and detach from the emotional angst—even for a moment. Reading about how others describe their transitions can also help you see your own transition better.

Other People's Stories

The following are private accounts of career transitions. In some, the author is currently in the transition; others are accounts of what happened in the past. Some transitions involve the change from a specific job; others are defined by a shift in the writer's overall career and life. Some are caused by sharp and well-defined endings, in Bridges's terms, such as being fired or laid off. Others began with more subtle shifts that are most clearly seen in retrospect. Whether voluntary or involuntary, you'll see that often the meaning of the change itself can develop—like a photograph—over time.

As you read my comments and these vignettes, try to understand how each situation may be similar or different to your own circumstances. As you develop your life, your work history will likely be comprised of many different changes and transitions. The meaning, importance, and scope of each can vary with your circumstances. Our discussion in chapter three will also begin to lift the veil on issues that confront many in work and life changes. It will foreshadow some important topics we'll examine in greater depth in later chapters.

First Job: Betrayal at Work

I've just realized that I've been in this transition for nine months. It must be a cycle I am finally coming out of. I needed to move forward, but it was very painful. My first professional job started with hope and cutting-edge technology—a new revenue management system. I did everything they asked; it didn't work. We had problems and I tried to solve them. The problems continued and I tried harder. At the end of an evaluation period, it was deemed my fault. How could I be betrayed like this? Working five to six days a week, twelve-plus hours a day, I was the model revenue manager and had always gotten good feedback. We were losing money. They came to fix the system, and when I returned from vacation they had assigned me to a new job—a demotion. Shame. Broken trust. I have no choice but to leave the company. I can see that this all undermined my confidence about work. I still miss my friends from there, but I'm feeling better now.

Yael, late twenties, employed the last three months in a new job as a sales manager in the hospitality industry

Sometimes a transition is best understood by looking back. Like Yael, we respond to the situation at hand, doing the best we can. Later, we can better see what we were up against and the impact of the changes on our life.

It is difficult to see young people confront betrayal or failure at work. Yet with personal feedback and good support, these challenges can be used to create new wisdom and empathy. Such experiences can strengthen leadership skills and clarify work values. For example, Yael may think, *I'd never do THAT to a subordinate of mine!*

A Burning Desire to . . . I'm Not Sure!

Transition into the unknown. Unknowing. This is my life; now what? I've prayed for guidance, for intervention, to ensure that I spend my life energy in a manner that makes a difference in the world but is perfectly in sync with my life, my heart's desire, my talents. What do I think? I *want* to be successful, to use the talents I have to bring a significant contribution to my firm. *I want to make a difference.* What does that look like? I don't rightly know.

Francis, early forties, currently a director of accounting in the financial services industry, salary $90,000

I don't have a career. Or, maybe I had a career and am ready for another. I've had twenty jobs since I was sixteen. Most were the make-do type. I'm tired of making do! And now I have the opportunity to do what's in my heart. "They," whoever *they* are, say, "If you do what you love the money will follow." Really? And what is it I love? How do I uncover that which I love? My life is half over now and yet I have another half to work and live. I wish I had a meaningful job.

Sofia, fifty-two, a temporary clerical worker with a background in teaching and graphic art

For many, work allows us to express our deepest purpose. If you are not aligned with your purpose—making a difference in a way that matters—you can find yourself struggling like Francis and Sofia. It's like having an intense drive that's blocked. Yet sometimes, we don't know what our purpose is. That makes the journey harder but the rewards even more profound.

A Simple Financial Equation?

However, if you think work or a transition at work means the same thing to everyone, you are mistaken. The relationship people have with work, what they want from it, and what it gives them can vary a lot. Here is an account from Teresa that illustrates this.

This is my transition: transition from having a job that provides money and health and retirement benefits to unemployment with no stream of income or fixed benefits.

Teresa, mid-thirties, laid off one month earlier, former senior manager for a communications consulting firm, salary $80,000

Your own understanding of what work means to you can also change, even within a couple of months. For example, shortly after losing a job, it can seem like you are looking for a job just for the money and benefits. Later, you may find your transition is heavily influenced by missing the opportunity to contribute and have coworkers.

My Real Passion Isn't My Job

What I love is writing screenplays, but I can do many different things to support myself. Employers just don't get that and here I am in transition again. I try to fit in and do my best. I know I did a good job and my employer liked me. But I don't think he understood me. Then when things get tough, I'm the first they let go.

Anabelle, thirty, formerly a secretary in a law firm, searching for a new job for two months

I've worked with a number of people whose calling wasn't in paid work. They're often musicians and artists whose real passion did not lead to well-paying jobs. Or they are people who just want to make a living so they can afford to do things that give them emotional employment: volunteering in their community, participating in political activism, or taking care of family members. They are reliable and capable workers but they somehow still fail to impress employers with their dedication. That makes them more vulnerable during layoffs and less attractive in a hiring process. And that makes it even more important for them to have the skills to effectively manage work transitions.

I Left but Am Still There

Here is where I am with my career: *I am stuck.* I'm in a job where I am respected, admired by my boss, where I know my way around the organizational labyrinth, where I could do it with my eyes closed, without thinking. After thirteen years, I know in my heart it is time to move on. I. What is holding me back? Why can't I just break free? Of all the times I wish this was one in which my job would be eliminated. But, it won't be. So, it's up to me. I don't want to make a mistake. I don't want to leave just to do the same thing somewhere else. So, I'm stuck. Each morning it is such an effort to get out of bed, figure out what I'm going to wear and drive to work. The only thing I enjoy is the trip down Lake Shore Drive, looking at the lake, the buildings, the green grass, the changing skyline, the daffodils along the road.

This past week I've been throwing out paper like mad— cleaning out files. I am detaching myself. Cleaning the space. I don't want the files anymore. It feels good. I want to keep throwing things away until I have the bare minimum to turn over to someone else, or to leave behind for whomever will take my place. I am thinking this is so much like the last year of teaching when I got bored but afraid. Fear holds me back. I wish I could just say the hell with it—I quit. And walk out.

Isabella, late forties, vice president of human resources, retail industry, salary $85,000

Fear is a feeling that echoes through the lives of many in transition that can completely stall movement. In some cases, it's because we get shackled by "golden handcuffs" and can't imagine a life without a job that pays a certain amount.

Lost Dreams

Realizing that life isn't going the way you had hoped can mark the ending of a dream and the beginning of a personal transition. When dreams end, we need to confront the reality, mourn the loss, and go on to create a new vision. This, of course, is *much* easier to say than do. I've worked with people whose lost dreams took many different forms. For example, you have wanted to be a professional athlete, but got injured in college; a doctor but, couldn't handle the sight of blood; or a politician, but you were gay and felt you couldn't be yourself and get elected. Or you spent your life believing you'd go into the family business, but Dad needed to sell it before you could start working. These may be realities you never imagined you'd have to confront, but you can.

The issue of whether or not to have children is very powerful for most women and many men. Like the dreams above, it structures our lives as well as our careers. When you realize you may not be able to have children, it can be a lost dream even if it was not a conscious dream. Some of our dreams are more conscious to us than others.

> I had been feeling less and less satisfied by work. I wasn't sure if PR had become boring or if work was even the problem at all. For so long, I think I'd assumed that at some point I'd stop working to raise a few children and then go back to work. So it seemed almost as if I was killing time. But after splitting up with my boyfriend I realized I was going to be supporting myself for a long time to come and kids might not be in the future. I needed to figure out what kind of life and career would make me happy.
>
> Erin, early forties, currently a public relations executive for a municipal public organization, salary $50,000

Mid-Life Misery: Having Everything and Feeling Depressed

We can be thrown into transition by simply reaching a goal we always wanted—finding the special job, raising our children, or finishing an important project. Achieving even your greatest goals will define natural endings. And after Endings comes the Neutral Zone where you may feel depressed.

> There was a time when I had what I thought I always wanted—a highly successful department in a major university, a department I started from scratch and for which I was the director. It was 1998 and the department was doing great and I had just published a textbook, which was absolutely a fabulous experience.
>
> I started to live the life that came with my goals. I was the chairman of a department and no longer teaching, which was what I did best. I was spending my days alone in my office, answering phones, hiring teachers, pushing papers, creating policy and products to grow the department. It was a successful, well-respected department in the college, highly recommended by students in word-of-mouth advertising.

Why was I falling into despair? Why did I dislike going to work?

Managing is hard. Something in me said that I should be stepping up to the plate. But I started to be terrified by the responsibility of it all. I started to cry a lot and feel depressed. I knew I needed help. I couldn't tell whether I was in chemical trouble or grieving the completion of my book, which had been four years of creativity and flow.

The book had been birthed. My children had been launched. My husband was distant, working through his own need for something that would give him the satisfaction he needed in his work life. Everyone said, "You're so privileged." I was. I am. No denying it. But my soul searched for meaning, well-being. I was so sad.

Gwyneth, fifty-six, professor and program director for a major university, salary $55,000

Sometimes we don't really know what we want until we get what we thought we wanted. Also, for many, the difference between leading and managing is an important one. They may love the leadership challenge of creating a vision and a new enterprise. However, once it's up and running, the task of managing it may be far less interesting.

Called Upon by a Deafening Noise

Dissatisfaction with your life and job are often intimately intertwined. You may know you need to make changes but feel powerless. It can start like a dull alarm going off while you are clinging to a deep sleep. You hear the sound but cannot rouse yourself to attend to it.

My transition began with an increasing dissatisfaction with my situation in life. It became a deafening noise in my mind—almost a constant noise of judgment and criticism. Everything in my life seemed to generate more noise. I knew I had to turn down the volume and tune into clearer reception.

This noise also evidenced itself in chronic job dissatisfaction. I had been working as an attorney for almost thirteen years without feeling any real success, not wanting to do the work required of me, not feeling engaged in my career at all. I felt very frustrated about money, and there was a feeling that my life was slipping away from me, that I had to gain control.

Aaron, mid-forties, partner in a law firm, undergoing a major career and life transition

Searching for Love, Money, and Myself

Making a commitment to find yourself as well as work that expresses you is a powerful decision. It may be easier to just be what others want you to be, especially if the external signs, like income, suggest you are successful.

Sometimes that job is like a band-aid holding together a life. Leaving the job can reveal aspects of yourself and your life that need to be healed or at least reconsidered. Many parts of your life can come under scrutiny when the job or career shifts. Losing or changing your job doesn't have to be a life-encompassing transition, but for some people it will be.

Well, when I quit my job, I knew it was the right thing—it always felt that way. But I didn't realize the abyss was waiting on the other side of the door. A lot of stuff came to the surface, still is, and still will about personal things, about my marriage, about my family, and things about myself I had never, ever faced, and had always avoided. And now the lack of a structured job left me with no distraction. I had to face myself, my own image of who I was, and I didn't like that. I couldn't face it. Quitting the job propelled me into a personal crisis whose magnitude I had no inkling of.

Hal, early forties, scientist, voluntarily left his organization nine months earlier

Redefining Work Success

Yes, as you grow and change, your values may also change. The work that fit you before can feel painfully at odds with the way you want to live now.

> I make more money in one year than my father made in the last ten years of his life. I find that money is really not the point any more. My family's health, having time with our twins, and not traveling all the time is much more important than I had imagined. My annual bonus is more than I ever dreamed I'd make in one year and yet, it isn't enough. I need a life and work that fits into it better than this. Life is short and they need me. And I need to be their Dad.
>
> Ivan, late forties, commodities trader, beginning the process of a job and career transition

Feeling Unaccomplished

Most people are driven to do well at work. Their self-esteem will suffer if they continually come up short according to their own or others' performance standards. You don't need to fail outright to feel like you have failed and you need to go elsewhere.

> My transition is caused by leaving my position as a technical writer and believing that my writing does not measure up as I once thought it did. I feel that I am at a crossroads and I don't know which path to take. Yet despite my flaws and rather unaccomplished history, I do believe that there is a correct choice for me to make. The problem is figuring out which choice is a correct one, and moving accordingly. At this juncture I want to make a smart choice, the right one.
>
> Jacob, mid-thirties, left his position as a technical writer at a software company three months ago for a career change

Yes, there is a smart choice for you, but not only one correct choice. Clients often describe themselves as losers when their work performance is just fine. Digging deeper, we often find their work just didn't reflect their sense of what is important. Believing there is only one correct career choice for you can create a barrier—perfectionism. We'll discuss that more in chapter three, "Recognize Key Challenges and Personal Barriers," and chapter five, "Condition Your Mind for Success."

Leaving a Mismatch—Again

It's not uncommon for the personal dynamics of a work situation to be repeated, creating serial transitions that are basically similar. For example, I've had clients who have had a bad boss or jealous co-workers in every work situation in their job history. As annoying as it is true, we often have a significant hand in creating these situations. And when we understand our part, we can begin to break the pattern.

> In graduate school there was a huge mismatch between my interests and those of my advisor. Although years later I enjoyed my job, the mismatch of my interests and the company's seems similar to the disparity between me and my advisor. My transition involves finding the next step and a better match for my life.
>
> Nathan, mid-forties, clinical psychologist who worked in health care and was laid off six months ago

Taking a Risk

Often in career decisions there is conflict between dull comfort and risk. Trying to do the right thing for yourself, you may confront loneliness, self-doubt, and other personal challenges. Career risk takes courage, and courage takes many forms.

> I like doing marketing research but I am afraid that my background doesn't really qualify me. I hope I can also learn new things but I am afraid that I will not get the chance to learn. I miss my family and my friends. I am homesick. Most of the time, I don't know why I stay here or why I moved here away from my family in Cleveland. I know I should do something

instead of watching TV, but I just can't help it. I think I'm escaping. I'm trying to avoid something.

Wung, late twenties, formerly a graduate research assistant, searching for a position in marketing research for the last three months

In the readings ahead, you will find tools to stay focused and evaluate which decisions are truly best for you.

Renovations at Home and at Work

I have yet to completely understand the interplay between house construction and career transition, but there is one. It's a complex relationship. Many people redo their careers and houses at the same time. Some get stuck in never-ending house renovation projects as well as stalled in making career changes. I do know that simple and uncluttered surroundings can help you stay focused. And a major concern for most people in transition is staying focused. More on that in chapter eight, "Create Structure to Stay Focused."

I lost my position in January of last year. It took several months to just get my life physically in order. I also felt a lot of stress due to an unfinished project at the house. While completing the project, I started answering ads and pursuing my job search with a recruiter, but never received an offer. I went back to college in the fall to take some graduate courses. Once I made that commitment to school, the house renovation started to fall into place.

Randy, late forties, project manager in manufacturing, unemployed for twenty-four months, looking for a new job for the last four months

Leaving a Bad Situation

Overall, the most successful career changes are motivated by moving *toward* something new and better. But I have also worked with a number of people whose movement was initially and for a long time about moving *away* from bad situations.

Here's my transition: My boss drove me nuts, why did he take credit for what I was doing? This liar even accepted money and gratitude letters for my work. I am so furious. Good thing this (bleep) got fired because of my resignation. They showed him the door exactly one month after I quit. I am so dumb though. Why did I quit?

Danny, early thirties, formerly in social work, looking for a new career for four months

Leaving a bad situation may be the best thing for you. Yet, like Danny, you may find it takes time to fully leave it behind in mind, body, and spirit. It will be important to work through intense emotional reactions so you can focus on the process of finding a new job. I'll help you with this in the chapters ahead, especially chapter six, "Let Emotions Be Your Strength."

Getting Fired and Finding Myself

Your sense of identity, strengths, potential, and goals can get distorted in situations that are bad for you. Being fired can feel like being dropped into a deep pool of cold water. Yet in time and with care, you will surface. You start to find yourself, feel better, and desire something better for your life.

I fear that in my life I have only seen the faces of others and I have made them my soul—seen through a carnival mirror. My transition is to become more open, honest, and true to myself. I want to see my face so that it becomes a mirror to my soul. I want to see me. To say hi. To learn who I am. To find out what gives me pleasure. To be okay.

Chandra, late thirties, attorney, terminated three months ago, just started to search for a new position

This type of transition has tremendous potential, but great care must be taken to relearn new messages about your self worth.

Confronting Devastating Career Loss

Some career losses strike deeper than others. I have worked with people who have suffered devastating personal and professional losses. They have been disbarred, had medical licenses revoked, and been defrocked as priests. I have found that the more significant the loss, the more potential there is for growth. Knowing there is a lesson in any situation, if we are open to it, is a formidable anchor.

> I am the first person in my family who had ever gone to college, and after my master's degree I wanted to get a Ph.D. I completed the course work and passed the qualifying exams for doctoral candidacy and tried to put together my proposal for the dissertation. Through a long series of events, my plans all fell apart. My dream was shattered. For a year, I couldn't talk about it without crying. I would wake up during the night sobbing in my sleep. I lost my focus and any sense of who I was. Believing there was something I could learn from that situation helped me survive. It was difficult.
>
> Marie, mid-forties, currently a marketing executive, salary $125,000

It's important to remember, devastating career losses provide the rarest opportunity to deepen our connection with our most authentic self.

Launching Issues: The Plight of the Twenties

The major task during our early to middle twenties is launching into the adult world. Like a plane trying to lift off a runway or a rocket shooting into the sky, we hope to get a good start on our journey. Young adults who aren't satisfied at work can feel tremendously unsettled: *Is this life? Am I a grown up? Am I doing okay?* They are also concerned with being on track, and compare themselves with their friends and former classmates. They wonder, *Am I successful? Is this good enough for this point?* They act as though people should be all at the same level, as in high school or college.

41

The story of my transition takes place over about one year. It was a personal transition as well as a career transition. My entire life changed. I was working full time as a caseworker for an arbitration firm while I applied to graduate school in psychology. When I wasn't accepted, I knew I needed to do something else I enjoyed. I had to spend nine months coming to find out what I could do and loved to do. My transition has had parts. I was first shifting to real estate and then to law—to be an attorney. I'm now studying for the LSAT and looking at law schools. Not knowing what I'd do caused me a great deal of anxiety and stress. Now I feel I'm going in the right direction.

Daniel, mid-twenties, account representative for a temporary agency, salary $30,000, looking for job and career change for the last nine months

Finishing the Degree: The Pressure of High Expectations

Finishing school is definitely a transition. It's an odd one, since the ending represented by earning the degree is usually such a happy accomplishment. We just want to go and live happily ever after and do well. Yet these high expectations can create stress. In addition to self-imposed pressure, there is often some level of pressure from family and friends.

Terrifying! That's how I'd best describe this transition. Graduating from my Master's program—actually being a professional counselor now—all that time, work, investment effort, but what now? What kind of counselor do I really want to be versus what I think I should be now in order to lead to a good, continuing step in the future? My own expectations of myself, others' expectations and perceptions are all entering in now. I've *always* had so much potential—will I live up to it? Do I want to?

At some points I feel like I am just lazy at heart—that I don't want to excel, to grow continually at something. Instead I just want to *be*. I just want to get a job that I'm happy with and enjoy in the present without looking at some future goal. But is that okay? Is that a waste of all my education, the potential that others have consistently identified in me? I don't want to disappoint my mentor and family or feel I didn't go as far as I could, but here I am at the first *real* juncture of my career—the chance to really make it count—and I'm terrified. I'm relying on faith and fate that the job I get and take will be the right one and will lead me on the proper path meant for me.

Jennifer, twenty-eight, completed graduate school in counseling psychology two months before

Am I Doing Okay? Struggling with Progress Markers

At any age, people can struggle with markers on where they are and where they should be. You may go through painful and punitive sessions reviewing and scolding yourself for your lack of progress. In the disorientation, and in your journey of transition, you have a new opportunity to create more meaningful markers. This is freedom, growth, and finding your own power.

This is my transition today: transition is frustrating. I know this is a bad way to look at my transition, but that is the way I see it. I think that if I had been more focused on my career in the past, that I would not be going through this transition now. I'd be in a job that I liked, was challenged by, and that was financially rewarding. In short, I'd be further along.

However, I also realize that there is no set path in life to follow, so maybe I'm not behind at all.

Michael, mid-thirties, consultant, financial services industry, unemployed two months, searching for a new career for one month

Just Wishing All This Was Over Twelve Months Ago

In the last couple of years, I have worked with a number of people, especially in the technology field, who never wanted to be in a job transition. Some had been through a number of job losses and had spent long periods of time finding new work. This path is often difficult. A special type of resilience is needed to manage one's way through a tough industry and economy with mind, body, and spirit intact. With good tools and disciplined actions, it is possible for you to develop that type of resilience.

> My transition started about fifteen months ago. My position as director of information systems was eliminated. The corporate headquarters felt it was a duplication of staff. This makes no sense with the increased importance of good security in our business. However, our office lost business last year and I knew something was going to happen somewhere, but I didn't really think they'd let me go. Even though they gave me severance, it's hard not to be angry. I had been there for over ten years—which is long for my field—but I did a good job for them. I'm divorced and have two daughters in college. I've had a number of interviews but no offers and lately not that many interviews. Companies can be so selective right now and require such specific experience. It's easy for them to find exactly the combination of skills and experience they need. My long tenure with one company has been limiting since I only worked with their systems, and other companies are more advanced. I've kept up on my training but don't have applied experience in the new technologies. Instead of that being helpful, it all feels like a big struggle right now.
>
> Paul, late forties, former director at a software company, salary $98,000

Still Hungry

If you believe that once you hit a certain age, like fifty, you will stop growing and wanting more in life, you really are mistaken. Research shows that some of our talents get better with age. Also, some people will have more stability and new courage to better take on new challenges. This can be especially true for women.

> I've known it was time to make a change for several years but I don't rush into changes. I contemplate them for a while first.

At my last job, I was clearly in the wrong institution. It always went against my grain—I never felt that I fit in or belonged there. But I had several job opportunities that led to my current job. In the meantime, I was growing as a person by experiencing new and increased responsibilities. The job change from that company to my current one was not completely satisfying, but an improvement.

I am in a technical job with a lot of people contact but I'm often restricted due to the nature of the work. I hunger for something more freewheeling. My daughter who is in marketing has been so supportive; she helps me take my goals more seriously.

Amanda, late fifties, customer services manager, salary $55,000, considering a career change

You can see that career transitions do come in many different shapes and sizes. Knowing your own transition story will give you power to begin transforming it. Like my group members, your career concerns, mishaps, and injuries don't need to define you or mire your spirit in negativity. By honoring yourself, you can get past what's difficult and be better for it. You can see that life is simpler than you thought and that you are much more heroic than you feel.

So, my surprise was realizing that my clients could transform their stories by writing them down and honoring them. However, they weren't the only ones who benefited from this process. Each time they wrote, I sat with them and did the same. With each and every one of my twenty groups, I'd explain the writing assignment, hit the stopwatch to time the exercise, and then write—and then write more. I wrote about losses and transitions I thought I had forgotten about years ago. I wrote about events whose imprints still marked my soul and consumed my deepest energies. While I didn't share my writings in the groups, I did show them to family and friends. The outcome was a gift I did not expect. It made me feel lighter, stronger, and clearer in ways that are difficult to fully describe.

Yes, I do believe in the power of knowing your career story and of writing down your feelings and experiences. That is why each chapter of this book ends with writing exercises. These will help you gain clarity about who you are, what you want and how to be sane, productive, and inspired in finding it.

WRITING REFLECTION EXERCISES

1. Could you identify with these stories as you read through them?
    If yes, which parts describe your transition?

2. Your Story: Take a moment and imagine telling someone outside
    your situation about your transition. Set an egg timer for five
    minutes. Write a description of your career or job transition.
    This could be in-depth with details, or an overview with just the
    essentials, or even a partial story. For example: What was the rea-
    son for the change? When did it begin? What were you doing
    when it started? Tell the story with yourself as the hero. Just
    write, don't stop. Write anything that comes to mind—even
    things you feel are stupid—just do it. When the timer rings,
    stop. Don't harass yourself if this was hard, you felt you didn't do
    it right, or you couldn't get much down. Congratulate yourself
    for your efforts! Try this more than once.

3. Read your story out loud to yourself. What did you learn?

4. Read your story out loud to an interested friend or family member.
    Have them just listen and repeat what they heard. What did you
    learn?

5. Ask your interested friend or family member to write and read
    their story. What did you learn?

.

CHAPTER THREE

RECOGNIZE KEY CHALLENGES AND PERSONAL BARRIERS

My biggest barrier? Questioning myself. I start the day thinking I really know what I want to do for my next career. By noon I lose all confidence and wonder what the hell I was thinking. When self-recrimination comes to call, it gets harder to be optimistic. If you don't believe in yourself, then you'll be pretty damn lucky to find others who will. Especially others who would stick their neck out and hire you.

Dawn, late thirties, formerly an architectural firm account executive, searching for a new career for one year, voluntarily left company six months ago

Self-criticism, indecision, impatience, and confusion. These are only a few of the internal barriers anyone can encounter. It's just that most people don't really talk about them openly and honestly with each other. Dawn is like many other people in transition who are confronting the challenge of what to do next in their careers. Her mind fills with self-recriminations that act as an internal barrier. They make it hard for her to have the confidence she needs to move ahead. She can become so absorbed in the recriminations that she can't see the practical steps that would make her feel stronger, such as undergoing interest testing or completing exercises in career guides. Or she may become like many people who work through career guides but whose barriers keep them from finding any sense of direction.

You need to recognize the natural challenges of career change as well as internal barriers that can unwittingly block your progress. Doing so can help you to inoculate yourself against the craziness that may be part of the emotional terrain, and to capitalize on the rare opportunities for growth that challenges and personal barriers can offer.

This chapter will help by giving you a simple formula for transcending difficulties, a framework for understanding how most internal barriers actually develop, a list of key challenges and barriers, and a special watch list of the most insidious barriers anyone can have. In the chaos of change, this foundation will help you regain a sense of personal control and create powerful tools for staying sane, productive, and inspired in your career transition.

HOW TO GET PAST WHAT'S DIFFICULT

Moving beyond the challenges and barriers may not be simple. However, if you take a learning attitude, it will be easier. Addressing your roadblocks can help you articulate your strengths and limitations more clearly, and thereby give you a more solid basis for creating the career and life you want. Here are the steps for overcoming both the barriers and challenges that get in your way.

Awareness

You must see things for what they are, in their most realistic light, and be honest with yourself. For example, you are undecided on a career path: *What shall I do? What is best for me? Hmmm, I've actually been thinking about what I could do for weeks now. I cultivate options and then find a way to put the brakes on any progress.* Knowing that you may be sabotaging yourself is essential to being able to stop it. If you can see it, you can begin to halt the cycle.

Acceptance

This means getting past the fight or denial about what is happening or has already happened, even if you don't like it. Once you accept the present circumstances that you have been struggling against, you regain a sense of control. *I feel plagued by indecision about my career right now. I really don't know what I want to do next. That's the way it is now for some reason.* You can waste a lot of time and energy avoiding the truth. Acceptance means you stop the fight—*It is what it is!*

Action

This means doing what you can to make a situation better for you. *I will work on my career assessment, take another test to better understand my style. Or, I will set this decision aside for a few days and go on to work on another of the chapters in this book for now.* Action is doing the next right thing based on a realistic understanding of the situation.

The impact of awareness and acceptance is profound. They can dissolve anxiety and increase your ability to take the next best action. They can make you wiser in ways that will affect your entire life. With some challenges in your transition, there may be nothing more or better you *can* do than to accept the situation and change what it means to you. For example, career indecision may represent a doorway to another level of honesty about yourself that you must pass through to move forward.

As you go through the list of challenges and barriers, keep in mind that my intent in this chapter is not to provide you with action solutions for each and every one of these. The purpose of chapters one through three is to make you smarter about the terrain of transition, your own transition story, and the obstacles you may confront. As you recognize your obstacles in this chapter, you can increase awareness and your ability to accept them. Additional action strategies will be presented in chapters four through nine. These will give you powerful suggestions from a number of different vantage points. These include your:

- behavioral style (chapter four, "Tap Into the Power of Style")
- mental patterns (chapter five, "Condition Your Mind for Success")
- emotions (chapter six, "Let Your Emotions Be Your Strength")
- intuition (chapter seven, "Cultivate Intuitive Guidance—Turn Up the Volume on that Little Voice")
- environment (chapter eight, "Create Structure to Stay Focused")
- circle of buddies and friends (chapter nine, "Help People Help You")

Before we go further, let's give some thought to exactly how those personal barriers begin to crop up in our lives.

HOW BARRIERS TAKE SHAPE

While certain challenges generally do come with the transition territory, internal barriers can emerge from a number of different factors. These include experiences with your parents, friends, and previous jobs. They may even have their roots in your behavioral style or environment. Be vigilant in looking for your own barriers in the stories of others. Also recognize that your own pattern of internal barriers will be as unique as your fingerprint. For example, Dawn may doubt her ability to do different work in the business world, but feel invincible as a mother. Or, you may have a tendency to wake up with self-recrimination but feel better as the day moves along.

One framework useful for understanding how internal barriers take shape comes from the work of Richard Bolles, author of the bestselling career book *What Color Is Your Parachute?* He presented this framework in a workshop I attended, and it was one of the most valuable things I learned.

Bolles sees us as continually trying to strike a dynamic balance between two selves. One he calls the Safe-Keeping Self. Others may refer to this as your ego or, more typically, mind. Practical and analytical, the Safe-Keeping Self is governed by logic and motivated by fear. Its job is to protect you and it will try to put the brakes on change because change entails risk to your safety. Pessimistic by nature, the Safe-Keeping Self tries to figure out what can go wrong. Intolerant of ambiguity and wanting things to go perfectly, it has a nasty habit of punishing you for deviations from the ideal. *Why didn't I major in something better in college? I'm thirty-seven years old and have no idea what to be when I grow up. I must be a failure.*

While the Safe-Keeping Self is valuable for refining a course of action once one is formulated, this critical nature can also deflate you long before you get to that point. I believe the Safe-Keeping Self is evident in many of the blocks that keep you from learning and moving forward. It's trying to keep you safe. And that's not a bad thing.

Bolles calls our other side the Experimental Self, since it reflects an appetite for risk, change, and creating new possibilities. The Experimental Self is your intuition—creative, optimistic, and positive. Unlike the Safe-Keeping Self, the Experimental Self thrives on ambiguity and a sense of play. It houses the most direct access to your spiritual purpose or calling. You need the Experimental Self for the creative parts of the transition, like connecting with your true passions, formulating the best career options, making a good marketing strategy, and pumping yourself up to stay the course.

Whereas the Safe-Keeping Self is driven by fear, the Experimental Self is driven by love and passion. In career development, you need both sides. You need logic, critical thinking, and practicality; but without creativity and a tolerance for uncertainty, you can get stuck. You can suffer paralysis by analysis—wanting to make it perfect before you can even start the work.

The first time I talk with new clients, I find most are steeped in their Safe-Keeping Self. In the midst of career uncertainty, the Safe-Keeping Self will have been conducting its own reign of terror. This Safe-Keeping Self dislikes change—sometimes even changes we have chosen. Most people will struggle with it, and some get completely stuck. Since the goal of your internal barriers is to protect you from risk and danger, you will be looking at the silhouette of the Safe-Keeping Self as we identify barriers.

AWARENESS TRAINING: IDENTIFYING YOUR ROADBLOCKS

This section will help you identify challenges and barriers in both the Endings and Neutral Zone of career change. You'll notice that many of the career transition challenges are interrelated and not easily separated. Keep an eye toward identifying which of these best describes the ways you are or have been stalled in your transition.

Getting Past What Happened

I don't seem to be able to make any progress. It just doesn't seem real. Last week I was working at my company and today I'm here in outplacement trying to figure out what to do with my life. How could they do this? I'm not angry—at least I don't think I am. Let's talk about something else. Why isn't this coaching going faster?

Kip, early fifties, manufacturing manager of fourteen years involved in a company-wide downsizing one week earlier

Often one of the biggest challenges in a transition is getting past how it came to be—endings. For example, when I work with clients in outplacement (company sponsored lay-off support), I know that I will *never* make any progress with them until they can tell me, in detail, what happened and how they feel about it. I used to think that sometimes this wasn't necessary. For example, when my clients saw it coming, were sophisticated and high-level employees, or had been laid off before. However, over time, I've learned it is *always* an error to skip over "what happened?"

If we do skip going over that question in depth, barriers are likely to appear. Frustrated Kip, above—not yet willing or able to explore it—is a good example. Common barriers I see include short attention span, boredom and preoccupation, inability to connect with people trying to help, difficulty remembering insights from previous sessions, no concentration for key tasks like résumé writing, lack of clarity on goals, aggressive behavior, passive-aggressive behavior, and lack of punctuality. In other words, my client won't be able to move forward effectively without airing out his story and the feelings that go with it.

When a career change does involve feelings of loss, these feelings can also create a strong personal barrier to making an emotional commitment to another job. It is as though your mind is a loyal and committed soldier protecting the wounded—you.

Can you deal with your feelings of loss once and for all? No, as we know, endings don't often happen that neatly. More typically, you'll confront a range of feelings at one point only to deal with them again later in a different way. In the following section are two challenges and potential barriers related to getting past what happened.

Refusing to Be a Victim

> You say it's good I have my son to live with now since I was fired? How would *you* like to live with your family, Diane? It's not fun! Even though I like him and it's a free place to stay, it's hard to share a computer, have my things in storage and not have my own space. This morning I went to one of those free job support groups you mentioned. Did you know they start at 7:45 a.m.? I told the director that there is no real reason to start this early since we are all unemployed. It's not like we have a job to go to afterward! I made an appointment with him next week so he can help me find a new job. I hope he has some good ideas.
>
> P. J., mid-forties, pharmaceutical executive, terminated from his position twelve months earlier

P. J. is a wonderful man who has been admired by many in his work and community. Right now, he is not someone whom many people are dying to help. Listening to his session above, you can see why. In many career transitions, the catalyst is an unfair situation. When unjust things happen to good people, they have a right to feel like victims. It is a significant challenge for everyone to avoid becoming a permanent victim and to not let your victim status present both internal and external barriers.

We can all carry bitterness and unresolved feelings from the past, even from years or decades earlier. Still, when we continue to carry these feelings, we are the ones who continue to suffer. Victims feel helpless. If you see yourself as a victim, it is difficult to recognize your true gifts and move ahead. To get through your transition, you need to find your own power and wisdom. Even as I write this, I know it may sound tired, trite, and much easier to say than to do.

55

But it's not. Dealing with your feelings *will* make you less vulnerable and more able to act productively.

Making Peace with Personal Failure

> Growing up, there was never anything I wanted to do except to be a doctor. In my right mind I know that stealing and using drugs was wrong. Now because of my own addictive behavior, I may never practice medicine again. It's been two months since the last review and I still don't know what will happen. This is a nightmare.
>
> Bart, thirty-three, former trauma physician, salary $125,000

Getting past what happened can involve different types of losses. What if your career losses are not someone else's doing and you are the one who screwed up? Experiencing personal failure is a challenge for everyone and we will all have some level of failure in our lives. Career failure is often hardest for those who have not had a history of failure in life. Still, I believe your failures will uncover the personal lessons you need to learn. Unfortunately, it's that way for all of us.

Hopefully Bart's precarious situation will push him into learning what he needs to know about himself and life. For example, sometimes people will blindly take care of others and forget how to take care of themselves. Their self-care can get distorted into risky or destructive actions like abusing drugs or alcohol. In trying to feel good, their actions may bring serious consequences. Bart's reckless road has the potential to bring him back to himself in a most profound way if he can honestly confront his addiction and his own needs. The chapters ahead will help you acquire tools and develop practices to take care of yourself and deal with personal failure. The suggestions under "Recognizing Troublesome Mind Patterns" in chapter five may be especially useful.

Confronting Career Amnesia

The biggest challenge is in convincing myself that I have a lot to offer. I know others look at my résumé and are impressed because I have real accomplishment and growth reflected there. But I feel as if it's not real, and if I don't really believe it myself, how can I possibly expect a prospective employer to? I'd like to be able to get over that, to recognize that I've done pretty well and can do even better in the future.

Erin, early forties, currently a public relations executive for a municipal public organization, salary $50,000

Even at its best, the middle phase of transition involves what I have begun to call "career amnesia." You may forget who you are, what you want, and why you are in this situation. Undergoing a thorough assessment of your skills, values, and passions can help you build a bridge to your next career move based on positive and realistic information about yourself. However, you may be like some of my clients who forget the insights they had even a week ago. I encourage them to summarize their career assets and goals on a three-by-five card and carry it around with them. It's easier to remember if you do something concrete like that. I've thought more than once that pinning it on a client's shirt could be a good idea. *Yes, you are smart, you DO have skills, you will get through this.*

Getting Past Feeling "Not Good Enough"

Even though this past job has been very successful, I am afraid underneath it all that I am not good enough to succeed in another job. I have to concentrate very hard to present myself as interested and outward so that I don't sink back into myself and show my fears.

Maggie, mid-fifties, laid off one month ago from her position of six years as a communications specialist

In the absence of positive information about themselves, which seems easiest to forget, people in transition can be incredibly hard on themselves. Most people seem to battle a great deal of self-doubt. If your self-confidence was low before the transition started, that can add to the self-doubt arising from the transition and create formidable barriers. Self-doubt can shoot you in the foot in countless ways. Detoxifying your negative emotions and attitude is so important in transition.

Being True to Yourself

Despite challenges such as the economy and job market, most people want to do work they feel passionate about. This is a major concern for many and reflects the drive for emotional employment. We want to be the best of who we are at work, exercise our favorite skills, and be recognized for them. This drive can be thwarted by a number of barriers that you may have experienced yourself. In the following sections are concerns I often hear that constitute barriers to being true to yourself.

What If the Door to My Passions Is Locked?

> It's so frustrating to me. I don't know how to get to it. I feel like there is something missing, something I am supposed to be doing, but I just don't know what it is!
>
> Gena, forty, securities analyst, left her firm three months earlier

I have met a number of people haunted by a tugging from deep within telling them they must do something different. Gena, above, is like Francis and even Sofia whom we met in chapter two. It's as though they have a message trapped inside them; the problem is they don't know how to access it. Their intuition is mute and they feel lost. *Do I want to go into sales or consulting? What really motivates me?* And often then they feel stupid because they have no instincts about how to proceed. I see this most with clients who have had to stuff their dreams and the knowledge of their special talents deep inside, and with those who never had a chance to figure out what their dreams and talents are.

The chapters that follow will help you get to know yourself better, particularly chapter seven, "Cultivate Intuitive Guidance: Turn Up the Volume on that Little Voice." The journey to increased awareness of your authentic strengths and passion requires small steps and consistent actions. However, the result will be that you feel much more alive. That's very much worth it, I think.

Not Sure Whose Little Voice I'm Hearing in There!

> Do I really know what I want from my life, or is it my parents' voices that I hear? Their expectations of me to be responsible and not just do something frivolous?
>
> Francis, early forties, currently a director of accounting in the financial services industry, salary $90,000

Yes, your intuition—that "little voice"—will guide you. However, sometimes in the process of finding your own voice, you can realize you've been listening to a chorus of other voices. This can be a big barrier. In fact, the desire to find your own voice may be the cause of your transition itself. You may need to get away from other influences to find your own way.

And just in case you believe that financial rewards will make you happy, Francis is proof that this is not always the case. Even in a tough economy, people still seek coaching to find work that better reflects their unique purpose.

But I Want to Fit in Too!

> My greatest challenges, dragons, and demons that get in the way of creating the career I want are feeling I should be doing something else, should be someone else, not allowing my instinctive, natural urges to emerge. Sulking that I'm not like others, sulking that I don't know what I want, when the truth is I'm not allowing myself to do, to be, that which is in my

heart—who I am. Self-denial in order to fit in a world of someone else's design.

Katrina, forty-three, college instructor, current salary mid $30s, has been working on a career change off and on for four years

Denying who you are and what you want is a barrier to being true to yourself. Yet acknowledging your true self feels risky. You may want to be unique and yet still be safe within the knowledge that you are like everyone else. That makes it harder to tune into your own voice. The task is to find the strength in who you are. Some especially valuable sections ahead are chapter four, "Tap Into the Power of Style," and a special section in chapter five called "Ideas for Strengthening Your Identity and Self-Esteem." Also be sure to do the writing reflections in chapter two on knowing your own story.

If I Can Do It, Is It Really a Strength?

I've always been able to make friends and have lots of relationships. I'm not sure that's a skill—it's just what I do. It's who I am.

Sidney, forty-seven, former senior manager with a major consulting firm, downsized two months earlier

Being true to yourself can be complicated by an inaccurate picture of your talents. Many people don't take into account their key skills. They believe that if it's easy for them, it's not a real strength. Examples could include problem solving, critical thinking, or networking. Minimizing your strengths is a barrier since you can't leverage what you can't see.

In creating a profile of your career strengths, it's important to get outside validation. Ask for feedback from people you know. It can save you lots of time and energy.

Managing the Uncertainty of It All

The toughest challenge I faced was the uncertainty of it all—not knowing where I would end up, not knowing if I was making the right decision to leave what I'd become so good at and worked so hard to set up. Where would I be in another several years? Would I bankrupt us with my search? Would I be better off? Would I carry my old problems with me?

Gwyneth, professor and director of a program for a major university, fifty-six years old, salary $55,000

This is the heart of what's hard in transition: the "between" space—between what was and what is, between what you want to do and what you are doing. Motivated by natural fear, your mind will be there analyzing, critiquing, and alerting you to any problems. This is fine, but don't get stuck in that mode. You need to draw from your intuitive self to feel positive and curious about the journey, to observe and learn. See fear as a signal to dig deeper and learn more about yourself and your situation.

Making Decisions

The biggest challenge of my transition is making forced choices between alternatives with pros and cons. I feel overwhelmed by too many possibilities and paths. It's hard when the path I choose is about the same as the one I didn't. What will I miss by leaving some path unexplored?

Nathan, mid-forties, clinical psychologist, unemployed for six months, started to work on making a career change during the last month

Indecision plagues many in transition. How can you make a decision, especially an important one, when you don't have all the facts, no matter how much research you have done?

If you had problems making decisions before your career transition, indecision may be a hallmark of this juncture too. Decisions

61

are commitments. If you don't like to make commitments about matters such as where you will live, or in your relationships, then work commitments may be difficult too. However, it isn't just making commitments that makes this juncture difficult.

I Don't Want to Just Settle, but I Need a Job!

There is a natural challenge in making career decisions, especially if you are out of work. You want to resist the temptation to settle for a mediocre position and you feel there may be a much better one for you if you keep looking. Yet, if you have been in transition for some time, you may just want income and for life to be predictable and steady.

> The biggest challenge in my job transition is to resist sub-par offers and sub-par companies when I am in such dire need of employment. I feel that if I take something just to take a job I will be in the same position in was in before I left—work hard, make no money, no room for advancement. I do not want to settle for something less than what I feel I am worth. I know I can be successful if given an opportunity to excel within a good organization.
>
> Wallace, early thirties, formerly a warehouse manager, voluntarily left his company and has been looking for a new position for a month

Working your way through the chapters ahead will help fortify your decision making ability. It will be especially useful to study "How to Strengthen Your Intuition" in chapter seven and even to work your way through the writing exercises in chapter two, "Know Your Own Story."

Putting Yourself Out There All the Time

> My biggest challenge is to keep moving forward, putting myself out there, being on my best behavior and looking the

right way. Calling people is what I like to do least of all. I'm not particularly fond of talking.

Hanna, early fifties, terminated from director-level health care position six months ago, salary $80,000's, actively seeking a new career for past three months

In a job transition, anyone you meet could be valuable in finding the position you want. In interviews, no matter how honest you are, you cannot completely be yourself, comfortable or candid. It can be taxing for everyone to have to be always "on."

Many people spend hours reviewing networking and employment interviews, trying to assess their performance. Extensive reviewing of conversations can become an obsession or barrier. Chapter five, "Condition Your Mind for Success," will help you deal with this and other mind patterns that can easily get the best of you.

Growing a New Skin

The transition is about finding a way to do what I like and make money at it. It is difficult to think about because I get confused. There are things embedded in this topic that are so hard for me to face head on: fear, my lack of self-identity and confidence, my image of myself as incompetent, etc. Very personal stuff.

Hal, early forties, scientist, voluntarily left his organization nine months ago

Transition and growth typically mean that what worked before does not work as well now. That is a fundamental challenge for everyone. It is possible to feel personal upheaval on a number of levels and to have a crisis of identity during transition. One analogy for this is that of an animal that grows a new skin. First, the old one gets mottled and tattered and then breaks apart. Meanwhile, with care, a new skin forms and shines through. It's a little sensitive and frail at first, but in time it is a better fit for your growing body. Career transition is a phenomenal opportunity for personal as well as professional growth and can feel like growing a new identity or skin. While it's uncomfortable at points, you don't need to get stuck in that feeling. Learning all you can will help you move along.

Living with Impatience

> I want this over with. I want the new job now.
>
> Isabella, late forties, employed internal human resources consultant, retail industry

Impatience is a powerful barrier to change. Not having a full concept of what it means to find a new job or career, many people describe themselves as being impatient or stuck when they have only begun the process. Or they have not done any of the footwork a transition requires. Often people just don't know the steps needed, or their level of fear keeps them from remembering or applying them. Impatience can burn up your energy and sap your spirit. This is one of the many dysfunctional mind patterns discussed in chapter five, "Condition Your Mind for Success." After reading it and practicing the techniques it offers, you'll be able to harness the energy of your own thinking much better.

Taking Care of Yourself While Making Do

> It has been most difficult to make choices due to lack of income. I need dental work. I need a regular doctor. I need a gynecological doctor. I need a podiatrist. I need clothes. I need new shoes. I need a PC and printer. I have to be patient. I have to make do. But though I don't want to make the non-Marcia decisions again of making some other person's dream come true, I also do not want to become sick.
>
> Marcia, early forties, unemployed for nine months from publishing industry position

One of the key tasks in a career transition is taking good care of yourself. It helps you learn and do your best. If you lack the financial resources to do that well or are intensely involved in a transition process, self-care can be a challenge. However, there are always some things you can do to take care of yourself even if you have to delay costly ones. Chapter eight, "Create Structure to Stay Focused," has a number of suggestions to help you nurture your energy and spirit that aren't costly. The section called "Using Feng Shui Principles" can jump-start your thinking. Also consider chapter nine, "Help People Help You." Maybe you don't need to do all the taking care of yourself by yourself.

Finding Time and Staying Sane While Still Working

One of the greatest challenges in this transition is trying to keep my sanity. When I set out to make the transition, I underestimated the amount of time truly involved. If something does not work right away I want to drop it. It feels as though it is a waste of time. I've had enough missteps. It is really hard to work at something without getting results real quick. This would be less of a problem if my current job did not make me want to walk out the door and never come back.

All of this makes me feel crazy. I argue with my girlfriend sometimes. It makes me a different person. My job fills me with an overpowering sense of dread five days out of the week. I spend most nights and weekends trying to escape the monumental upheaval. Keeping everything sane is top priority for me.

Daniel, mid-twenties, account representative for a temporary agency, salary $30,000, looking for job and career change for the last nine months

Trying to make a career change while working full time presents its own challenges. Certainly financial security from having a job is beneficial. But there can also be a persistent sense of chaos and disorganization from lack of time and feeling half-there in a situation that doesn't fit. This can become a barrier to positive movement.

Chapter eight is specifically designed to help you with the sense of chaos many people in transition experience.

Staying with It—Maintaining Positive and Focused Energy

The biggest challenge is keeping my energy level up and directing myself to a goal that will lead me back to employment. I have experienced several periods of depression and lost significant energy during those periods.

Randy, late forties, project manager and engineer in manufacturing, unemployed for twenty-four months, looking for a new job for the last four months

It is much easier to keep busy doing my job, working around the house and in the garden, and socializing than to do the really hard thinking that is necessary.

Brita, early fifties, employed project manager for a small manufacturing firm, salary $40,000s, has been searching six months for a new position

The hardest thing has been to keep at it every day, whether it is researching, generating leads, getting interviews, or following up. I know I can do better. But do things ever get better? Too many lights at the end of the tunnel seem to turn into freight trains.

Carlo, late forties, salary $65,000, currently a staff assistant, has been looking for a new position for ten months

A key difficulty most people will face, whether employed or not, is staying focused on the task of creating a better work situation. The lack of structure needed to create good momentum is often the crux of the issue. Procrastination and paralysis are reactions to fear, but these barriers can stall your progress.

Handling Rejection

The biggest challenge is to accept rejection and not to deny myself. Being rejected is normal. That's what I was told. But rejection still makes me depressed. I don't know how long this is going to take. I tell myself that being rejected is the necessary process to go through.

Wung, late twenties, formerly a graduate research assistant, searching for a position in marketing research for the last three months

Rejection is part of any career transition process but it can be tough, especially in a difficult job market. "Yes" or "no" can mean the difference between security and happiness or working your way through more frustration and uncertainty. Rejection also can present a significant challenge to your identity. Low self-esteem can make this even more difficult.

THREE MAJOR BARRIERS GUARANTEED TO MAKE EVERYTHING WORSE

I'm sure by now you have an idea of the barriers that can hold you back as you face the challenges of career transition. This section describes three very insidious barriers. Be on special alert for these.

Infinite Lack

Nothing I do will make a difference. What's the use of working at this? I can't make a living and will never get hired doing what I want anyway. I'm just like a lot of other people whose life savings are getting eaten away while these overpaid higher-ups walked away from the situation with our money and no accountability. It's criminal. Nothing will ever change. I'm poor and will always be that way.

Ralph, fifty-four, let go four months earlier from his position as a staff accountant for a major airline

Infinite lack is my term for a state that is different from depression and a bad mood. It is when a lack of your sense of self, of your future, of having any real effect on your world marinates and then simmers in a horrendous absence of possibility. You can feel it seep into your mind as you emerge from the safety of sleep. You have a sense of doom, sadness, and bleakness about your future, no matter how much money or love you have. You carry this thick sense of poorness and lack; it exudes from you. Your world and life is colored by it. It is hard to make a creative change, or any type of change, in this frame of mind. Infinite lack is a true insidious barrier.

I've met people of all means in this state. For example, Gina, a client who could easily cover her rather luxurious lifestyle without a job for up to six months, who had a nice boyfriend, supportive parents, her own home, and complete health except for a runner's injury. Yet she fell into this deep sense of lacking. She believed she had no future and there was nothing she could do. This is a state of mind that you can, and in fact must, get yourself out of.

Jobless Paranoia

If he believes her, what kind of person is he? It's so hard when the world is always against you.

Max, mid-forties, brand manager who has been looking for a position for almost seven months after his department was down-sized

An executive coaching group I conducted came up with the term "jobless paranoia." It describes a pattern of thinking that makes connections between events that are realistically improbable. The insidious aspect is that you can't always see what is unrealistic in career change. Example: You want a specific job and think you have it. Your skills are a good fit and the hiring manager has told you that. He said he'd call to confirm hiring details in two days. Three days pass and he hasn't called. You begin to think that another friend recently hired by this same company has said something negative about you. Maybe she never really liked you and is jealous since you are more talented. However, the reality is probably: a) she doesn't even know you applied; b) she isn't jealous of you; or c) the manager hasn't ever talked with her, let alone about you. Still, your poor mind is working overtime: *How could this happen?* You worry you will never get ahead or hired for anything you really want. *He must be a creep if he believes her and doesn't hire me.* Your thinking goes on and on. By the fourth day, the manager calls. He says he's sorry—he got called out of the office for a couple days—and offers you the job. You're not even sure you want it anymore. You get yourself in a state like Max's, thinking everyone's out to get you.

Jobless paranoia can result from a combination of elements gone awry—including pessimism, self-critical thinking, and low self-esteem—blended with an unfortunate aspect of career change: unpredictable timelines. Your creative side is making a story of connections where there are none. If this describes you, stop and get your thinking on a better track. Chapter five, "Condition Your Mind for Success," will help you get out of this thinking.

In our coaching group, members would sometimes vent frustrations about these unjust and agonizing situations that occurred. From time to time, the group would just nod in unison and say *jobless paranoia.* It can be a relief to know it's in your mind and probably not real.

Sex, Lies, Alcohol, and Chocolate

I wanted to avoid drinking with my friends for a while but I can't even remember what time I got home. I slept with who? Oh no! . . . I said I'd do what for whom, by *when?*

Bernie, early thirties, former general contractor looking four months for a position that better suits his talents

In limbo, we can encounter our tendency for obsessive thinking and its close kin, compulsive behavior. The sequence generally works like this: unable to find satisfaction in work or life, you turn to substances. That, in itself, is not necessarily a bad thing. Unless you're an alcoholic, treating yourself to a nice dinner and a glass of wine is an excellent comfort after a hard day. But if you find yourself drinking at every lunch or if lunch turns into the rest of the day, you have a problem.

The most difficult part of an addictive pattern is not that we deceive others. It's that we deceive ourselves. Our minds become filled with obsessive desires and the shame that follows in trying to fill the emptiness with substances: *I ate the whole thing?* Eating disorders are rampant in our culture. Many addictions involve people-pleasing—making everyone else happy except ourselves.

If you spot your own obsessive and compulsive patterns above, you're not alone. If you feel powerless to stop addictive behavior, get help. Psychotherapy or one of the number of twelve-step programs built on Alcoholics Anonymous, such as Overeaters, Debtors, and Narcotics Anonymous, have helped millions and could also help you.

Challenges and barriers will naturally emerge in your career transition. Recognizing them will help you begin to transform them. The sequence to transforming what's difficult is awareness, acceptance, and action. It would be best if we could immediately recognize all our own barriers, and yet some are so insidiously ingrained in us that that would be very difficult. One major way to get a better view of your own barriers, as well as natural gifts, is to understand your behavioral style. We'll discuss that in chapter four, "Tap into the Power of Style."

WRITING REFLECTION EXERCISES

1. Which of the quotes above did you most identify with? Why?

2. List and describe the challenges and barriers you are currently facing in your transition.

3. What are the costs of your most dominant personal barriers? How do they affect you and your progress?

4. On a scale of one to ten, rate your degree of awareness and then acceptance for each of the challenges and barriers you listed above.

5. How might you increase your acceptance of your challenges and barriers?

CHAPTER FOUR

TAP INTO THE POWER OF STYLE

All I said was: "So, what's keeping you from hiring me right now? I can start in two weeks." If we really were such a great fit, it seemed best to just be direct and ask the question. He looked surprised, put his head down, and said he'd call after he finished interviewing the others. I never heard back from him and he hasn't taken any of my calls. That's my style—what you see is what you get. Apparently he's not quite as honest.

Raymond, thirty-eight, former sales manager from a wine and spirits distributor, unemployed for three months after a corporate downsizing, salary $90,000

I f you're like most people, while reading the last chapter you spotted at least a few insidious barriers that could keep you from moving toward the work you love. You may have other barriers that will be difficult to identify by yourself, in the same way you can't see your nose or the back of your head without a mirror. The good news is that some internal barriers are just natural consequences of our behavioral style, which can be much easier to pinpoint. As with our outspoken Raymond above, your behavioral style can also create real *external* obstacles to finding emotional employment. Some people are put off by Raymond's "honest" style.

Your behavioral style can also include natural talents you would do well to feature in future work, talents so instinctual you may believe everyone has them. That's another area where you don't want to have blind spots. In managing your career, doing what comes naturally is a cornerstone of success. So settle into chapter four with your best learning attitude. Learning to tap into the power of style is very important. To begin, exactly what is behavioral style?

BEHAVIORAL STYLE AND PERSONAL PARADIGMS

Sometimes when I sit and listen to my clients talk about what they did and what happened, I feel perplexed. What they did made such perfect sense I can hardly believe that, for example, it got them in trouble at work or didn't land them the job. Then I remember that we all have good reasons for what we do. We almost always make sense to ourselves. And yet, that gets us to the very heart of the issue. We see the world and act in terms of our own perceptions and personal paradigms. However, these perceptions are not necessarily shared by others. Within Raymond's world view, he was doing the right thing. Yet what he thought was honest could be considered inappropriate, brazen, or even rude by his interviewer.

As we discussed in chapter one, to be successful in our lives we must refine our views to better reflect how the world actually works. We all need to get past the idea that our personal paradigms are how everyone else thinks, and to cultivate deeper awareness of the limits of our world view. Behavioral style reflects one set of personal paradigms.

We each have a behavioral style. Basically, there are two methods to sharpen your understanding of your own style: 1) read about different styles and how they work and 2) take tests or other feedback instruments to form an objective assessment. Using both methods is a good idea.

Early in my practice, I didn't talk much about behavioral style or rely on tests or other assessment tools. I had worked with a number of clients who resisted this, saying they didn't want to be labeled or reduced to a category. Despite my training, I found their concern rather compelling, yet over time, it felt limiting to shy away from using these concepts and tools.

To understand ourselves, most of us do benefit from categories or "buckets" to help sort and simplify the complexity. We are all definitely unique in terms of genetics, personality traits, and background experiences. And behavioral style is not the whole picture. It would be a mistake to proceed as though it is. However, having a basic language to describe the style of our actions in important situations is tremendously helpful. Overall, high-quality assessment tools can provide valuable mirrors. They allow you to go beyond your blind spots and to see and identify aspects of yourself you would not ordinarily be able to see.

Your behavioral style can serve to either move you in your direction of choice or slam on the brakes. This chapter will help you develop a deeper understanding about what behavioral style is, pinpoint strengths and limitations of your own style, and use your insights to more easily create working relationships. That includes the relationships you will need whether you are looking for a job or already have one. Further, this chapter can increase your emotional intelligence, not just at work but in every area of your life.

WHICH FRAMEWORK? PERCEPTION MAY BE EVERYTHING

While there are a number of different frameworks for understanding behavior style, the one I find most useful for career transition was developed by Dr. William Moulton Marston in the 1920s. Marston, who also invented the lie detector, believed that our behavioral style is determined by how we see a given situation, such as an interview, a specific relationship, or the current work environment.

From the first time I heard about Marston's model, it made intuitive sense to me and filled an important gap I had found. Often when I used personality tools like the popular Myers Briggs Type Indicator (MBTI) my clients would say, "Diane, this describes how I act at work, but it's not me at home." The MBTI is useful for making a decision about what type of career you should pursue. It answers the question: Does the job match your core personality or true colors? Marston's model is designed to reflect situational behavior, and that's the stuff that can help you *through* the journey to get that job.

Marston identifies two basic factors that work together to determine our behavior. One is how *favorable*—how comforting or threatening—we perceive the specific situation to be. For example, you may feel psychologically or even physically threatened sitting with an abusive boss or walking through a dark alley in a high-crime neighborhood. In the language of chapter three, this means you are being motivated by some level of fear. Or you may feel safe and comfortable chatting with a generous mentor or at a gathering of old friends—a lack of fear.

The second factor is of the degree of *control* you feel over the environment. Are you more or less powerful than the key elements of the situation? For example, if your abusive boss has the last word on everything and you have no recourse, you will be likely to perceive your power in the situation as low. On the other hand, if your boss is on her last day of work since she is being fired, you could view your power as high.

THE FOUR DIMENSIONS OF THE DISC® MODEL

In Marston's theory, these two factors come together to create four basic patterns of responses to a situation; this is called the DISC model. These four patterns are considered dimensions of behavior. While everyone will show some degree of each of these four dimensions in their actions, people are typically described in terms of their highest one or two—D (Dominance), I (Influence), S (Steadiness), or C (Conscientiousness). As you read each of the four behavioral dimensions in depth, try to identify which best describes your style at work.

Dominance: Do It My Way . . . Now!

First is Dominance (D). This behavioral pattern is found in those who view the situation as unfavorable, but see themselves as more powerful than the situation. They believe they can and need to make changes. They are likely to be natural leaders—aggressive, goal directed, and decisive. They are motivated to get control and create results. Like Raymond, their motto is: *What you see is what you get.* People with high Dominance patterns—we'll call them High D—may run the risk of others feeling on the defensive or just wanting to escape their unvarnished directness. If you understand the concept of behavioral style, you will know that this Dominance pattern is not personal. Recognizing this is a relief when you encounter the High D style. And you also may need to remind yourself that we all have our own styles in certain environments and good reasons for them. If we were to characterize this style in terms of the animal kingdom, High D would be an eagle. Powerful, often distant, and focused on what it wants.

Influence: We're in This Together—and It's Fun!

The second dimension is called Influence (I). This behavioral pattern is found in those who view the environment as favorable. They are not threatened. They also see themselves as more powerful than the situation. People high on the I dimension tend to be talkative, friendly, and fun to be around. Not threatened, they can enjoy others as a source of pleasure and exert their power to bring people together toward a common good. The High I style is typically more focused on relationships than tasks. Each style has its own down side. While the High D profile may distance others with an unvarnished directness, those with High I style may not be taken seriously in some situations. While they may enjoy the creative start-up phase of new projects, follow-through is not a hallmark of the High I behavioral pattern. Flashy, attention-seeking, and popular, this style is most like a peacock.

Steadiness: Easy Does It, Don't Rock My Boat!

The third dimension is Steadiness (S). This is found with people who view the situation as favorable and their sense of power in it as low. Since the situation is viewed as favorable, they have no need to initiate changes. This is fine, since they don't see themselves as able to effect change easily anyway. In fact, content with the status quo, they tend to resist change. These are the steady contributors in organizations who are found at all levels. Their style is generally respectful of others with whom they feel little or no threat. It's often said that while people with the High D profile are lying awake at night thinking of all the changes they will make at work, High S people are awake thinking of how to stop them. Of course, the actions of the High S are likely to be far less direct.

The typical behavior of High S profiles is patient, accepting, and cooperative. I once worked with a High S in a large manufacturing firm who very much wanted to move out of her division—and soon! The reason, though, was very consistent with her profile; her boss had been disloyal to her. Loyalty is a cardinal value of the High S profile. Warm and reliable, this behavioral style could be characterized best as a teddy bear.

Conscientiousness: I'm Doing This the Right Way!

The fourth dimension is called Conscientiousness (C), and reflects perceptions of low power and high unfavorableness. In other words, these people believe the situation is threatening and they can do little or nothing to change it. This pattern is characterized by a cautious, indirect, analytical, aloof, and exacting approach. Natural strengths of the High C profile are being able to understand, adhere to, and create structures. The High C approach is to get it right to ensure their safety. They want to know all the rules and policies and how to follow them so they won't get in trouble. Diplomatic and objective, they can also be perceived as too detail-oriented, picky, and critical. Their presence is similar to that of a porcupine. Maybe not the loudest members of the human zoo, but you'll know when you've threatened them.

The Self-Fulfilling Prophecy and Your Behavioral Style

One question you may be asking right now is: Do our perceptions and behavioral styles shift radically in different situations? Or, do we really have only one basic way of being defined by these four dimensions? Can you, for example, act differently at work, where you feel threatened, than at home, where you are safe, happy, and accepted? Answer: I'm not entirely sure. Marston did see us as more flexible than some of my clients seem to be. Even in radically different situations, many believe their behavioral style (such as High D or High I) is their natural style. It's probably the case that some people are more adaptable than others and can adapt their style more across situations. Being flexible so that you can adapt your behavioral style to meet the needs of a situation is a good thing in life as well as work. For example, when physically threatened, we might all benefit from having some of Raymond's no-nonsense directness.

One truth is that your perceptions and behavior can create a certain type of situation; your beliefs can become self-fulfilling prophecies. Example one: You are a High I manager with a new employee. You love people and being around them. You treat your new subordinate as a friend, show her the ropes, and give her plenty of positive feedback. You are happy she is on board and keep her in the loop on everything important to her job. Do you think this will create a favorable situation for you? One where you have power to make a difference? Yes. And yes. Your employee is much more likely to be a trusted and cooperative employee when treated well. Your belief that this situation is favorable is confirmed by the way she and other employees are acting. You are more likely to have power when people like and respect you.

Example two: You are a High D manager and go home to find your spouse has made a wonderful dinner featuring your favorite food. The laundry is all done, the table is set, and the house is sparkling clean. Working from the High D perspective, you may be more suspicious than honored. Reflecting your world view, you ask, "Sooo, did you wreck the car again?" Do you think that would create an unfavorable situation? One where you have influence (albeit negative)? Yes. And yes, again.

Keep in mind that your perceptions and behavior will create situations for you in the process of your career change—in interviewing, networking, and more. So how can you make that insight work for you as you move along your journey? To better understand your style, let's explore how it may create strengths as well as barriers.

CREATING POWER FOR YOUR CAREER TRANSITION

As you saw in chapter three, it is often difficult to identify your own internal barriers. Again, the eye can't see the face without a mirror. However, it can be easier to first identify your behavioral style, and then ask yourself whether the strengths and internal barriers usually associated with it describe you. In some situations, our strengths can turn into limitations or sabotage our best efforts.

Here are some of the barriers and strengths that I've seen with the different behavioral styles. Think about which of these apply to you. And if you can't see yourself that clearly, ask a friend's opinion or go to my website (www.back-in-control.com) and complete the

DISC online assessment. No one needs blind spots in navigating career transition!

Dominance: Finding Control When You've Lost Your Way

> The hardest part of my career transition was having others help me when I was down. I am so used to being the one in control. I really thought I could sort this out myself. I waited six weeks after I left my company to tell my wife about it. At first, I just went downtown to the outplacement office instead of to the office. I wanted to solve this myself and keep her out of it. Overall I hated not knowing how this would work out and when. The whole thing was an adjustment.
>
> Raymond, thirty-eight, former sales manager for a wine and spirits distributor, unemployed for three months after a corporate downsizing, salary $90,000

Those with the High D style are likely to be able to put themselves out there, making calls, doing interviews, and thinking big. They may be inclined to handle the independent work required in searching for a new job and to appear self-confident. However, in a career transition, especially if they have lost their job, they are likely to feel out of control. If you identify with the High D style, this lack of control can throw you off kilter. You can feel very vulnerable and want to withdraw or strike out.

I've known many hard-driving executives who have suffered miserably when they moved off the center of everyone's radar screen. Since they are no longer in charge at work, they need to look hard for other ways to be in charge. This is positive if they find other activities like volunteering at a not-for-profit, or coaching their children's teams. But the need to be in control can also take some unhealthy turns if they end up turning all this dominance on their significant others, family, and friends. Your relationships will suffer if you start lashing out or suddenly bossing people in your personal life. If this happens with you, find more constructive ways to be in control. Identify the areas in your life you *can* control and leave the rest alone. Don't be a victim of your style.

Another limitation of this style is: *It's my way or the highway.* While confident of their strength, those with the High D style are still motivated by threat and fear. The process needed to create and work with career possibilities can be short-circuited by the demanding impatience of the High D profile. Looking for certainties when there are only possibilities can also short-circuit creative energy. If the High D profile describes you, be sure to coach yourself to see career change as a process. You'll have a number of steps to take; you'll want to save your energy and work through them with deliberateness.

If you have a High D profile, watch your manner with secretaries and others on the way to the hiring managers. Because of your own natural strengths, you could unwittingly come off as pushy, arrogant, or controlling.

Letting others lead may not come naturally. Recently, I was working with a High D sales manager who had been laid off a year ago. He had been actively searching for a new job for twelve months. His wife suggested he contact a counselor since she had some concerns with the way he presented himself. He always made it to the last round of interviews but was never offered the job. Finally, giving up his pride, he came in for coaching. Giving feedback to someone vulnerable who needs to be in control is an art I've spent my career trying to perfect—not always with perfect results. I pointed out ways in which his natural strengths in taking charge (which could also be seen as aggressive) may have become amplified by his frustration with being in transition and had started to work against him. I told him that living with his considerable power and abilities right now was like having a race horse in the basement. (This was true.) I assured him that, for now, he could use these personal strengths and knowledge to manage his reactions. Later, he could better use these skills. He took my feedback well because he considered me an expert he had hired so he could do better. I was working for him, like an employee. This way of framing the coaching relationship and my effort to empower him allowed him to use the input. As a High I myself, if it meant I could help him, I was fine with it.

One final thought: As a High D you may feel it is good to be candid, like Raymond at the beginning of the chapter. However, unless you are talking with another High D, it may be wise to temper your style. Building trust with people who are different from you involves an understanding of their personal paradigms. More on this later.

Influence: When It's Hard to Make Others Happy

> I've stayed on my current job for far too long. I love the people but the situation is killing me. We talk about it all the time but none of us has had the courage to leave. My best scenario would be if we all left at the same time. I also feel a commitment to my customers. Who will take care of them? My blood pressure is high from worrying about whether I can cash my check without it bouncing. I need to take care of myself better than I do.
>
> Charlotte, fifty two, staff writer for a trade magazine

If you have a High I profile, it is likely you have unique strengths in developing personal relationships in job situations you enjoy as well as those you don't. This can make leaving a job that's not good for you a difficult decision. While many may struggle with networking, if your behavioral profile is High I, you probably will not. This is an excellent strength in a career transition because having a wide circle of connections can create more possibilities. Your inner barriers are likely to be that you want to please others and have difficulty figuring out what's best for yourself. Striving for acceptance and recognition, you may find it easier to hear the voices of others than your own. Decision-making may not come easily. Further, rejection, a natural part of securing a new position, may be especially difficult. If this is you, I recommend working hard on the methods that focus you on your own story and ground you in your strengths and intuition—chapters two and seven.

Enjoying people, you are probably happiest surrounded by others or working on a team on a variety of tasks. If you're without a job, especially if you are laid off or fired, the lack of contact with others may leave you feeling lonely and unmotivated. You may need to work harder than some on staying focused, especially on the task-oriented parts of the transition, such as finding information about companies, careers, or job leads. Balancing emotions is also likely to be more of a challenge for you than it is for some others.

The creative process in career change may come more easily than applying logic and organization to the ideas you generate. For instance, you are likely to be more energized to start projects—such as research or letters—than to do them. You may have more ideas than specific plans. At their worst, High I's are like happy comets, flying around without getting much done. If you consider yourself a High I, finding or creating a support group to help you stay on track during your transition could be an excellent idea.

Steadiness: When Change Is *Not* Your Favorite Activity

> I have a system for finding a new career. I'm reading *What Color Is Your Parachute?* to research the best steps and I've read several other books too. I spend two hours a day online and am taking all the tests I can at my alumni office. I've been working on it like this all summer. The routine keeps me going.
>
> Michael, mid-thirties, consultant, financial services industry, unemployed two months, searching for a new career for one month

If you are high on the S dimension, you are Steady. Once you have dealt with any sudden or unpredicted change like being laid off or fired, it will be important for you to make a plan and establish a routine. While the High I profile may struggle with keeping a routine, once you've established a schedule, sticking to it will be a strength for you. Your need for consistency will help you stay on track with the activities of career change. On the other hand, your need for routine could be a hindrance. For example, as a High S you may not want to schedule a job interview if it throws off the plans you made for the week, even though getting job interviews is a major goal.

If you are stuck in your transition and believe your profile is High S, you'll probably need to counteract your natural tendency to avoid a change. High S's can get complacent and not take the initiative to create genuine opportunities. You are likely to do more homework on yourself, on new options, and on companies than some of the other types, and yet not step up to the plate, arrange interviews, or otherwise go after situations that could turn into a new job. It's as though you can't digest the fact that you are in charge of making the change. You are more concerned about process than outcomes and tend to be indecisive. Also, your loyalty to others and desire for security may keep you from making decisions in your own best interests. It may not be easy for you to push yourself out there, but it is necessary.

As an S, you are likely to handle relationships well. Your respectful, calm, and amiable manner is usually well received. But one limitation of this casual and warm style is that it may not allow you to be seen as aggressive enough. If you want to work in competitive environments, you may have to convince others that despite your easy-going nature, you can succeed.

Conscientiousness: Can You Tell Me Exactly How Long Transition Lasts?

I know there is a perfect job for me out there. I just need to find it. I'm organized and have studied all the books, so I know I'm doing this right. It's just a matter of time. I calculate that if it takes a month for every $10,000 I want to make, I'll have a job by June. If not, I'll still keep getting certifications in my field. This will show my high level of expertise and I'll be able to command a higher salary.

Jacob, mid-thirties, left his position as a technical writer for a software company three months ago for a career change

If you identify with the High C behavioral style, your strengths probably include your ambition to learn all the facts about how to make your career change successful. Like High S, you perceive that you do not have power to shape the situation directly, so you have the tendency to engage in careful planning and organizing. There is a different feeling to the High C approach, however. High C's are more exacting and driven to get it right. You are typically quite meticulous in understanding test results, doing the exercises from the career manuals, and researching job options. You want to adhere to high standards, be objective in your process, and do this right. You will learn, organize, and persevere, usually on your own.

As a High C, you are likely to be plagued by internal barriers of the Safe-Keeping Self: perfectionism, procrastination, and even paralysis. You need to remind yourself that you can't do a career change perfectly, and you should carefully work your way through chapter five on conditioning your mind for success. Typically you deal with overwhelmed people in companies who don't respond as you want. Developing a new career choice or job is a creative process. That entails a certain chaos, which is often uncomfortable for those with High C profiles. There is not just one correct career, there may be several. Further, many great careers have evolved from jobs that didn't seem to fit that well at first.

Familiar comments from my High C clients:

What am I supposed to talk about with you as my coach? I want to know the rules so I can do "being coached" right.

Exactly what are these tests telling me? What's the correct direction from these results?

It's not supposed to happen this way! Those companies should be more organized and get back in touch with me when they said they would!

How could they even not acknowledge my résumé, that's downright rude of them. Why couldn't they just send me a rejection letter—I can't believe this.

Not that a High C client would typically do more than complain to their coach! When disappointed by others, High C's are more likely to do a slow and silent burn. Whether you express it or not, if you are overly concerned about the correctness of the actions of others while navigating your career change, let me give you some good advice: Stop! Let it go. Your concern can make you feel crazy and be very unproductive. You have better ways to spend your energy.

For interviews, if you are a High C career changer, you'll probably want to read everything on the job and company to understand the potential opportunity very well. However, it's not just the facts that will be important in the interview—personal chemistry can make a big difference in whether or not you are hired. So, unless you're with a High C interviewer or can flex your style to match the interviewer's style, things may not go that well. I suggest doing enough research so you can relax, and making sure that part of your research is on how to communicate with others—like your interviewer perhaps—who have different styles. And that's what we'll be discussing next.

All four behavioral styles have their own strengths and barriers. And your own style, whether it is situational or remains constant, will have elements of each of the four dimensions. Don't resign yourself to limitations by saying: *Okay, that's my barrier since I am a D, I, S, or C.* Use these descriptions to understand yourself *and* to learn where you need to draw from the strengths of others in your transition. The people around you will have strengths you need to draw upon to make progress. Remember that our sequence for transforming limitations is awareness, acceptance, and then action.

Using Style to Become More Emotionally Intelligent in Your Transition Relationships

In a career transition, as in life, you do need to develop and maintain relationships. Having a strong network of people—friends, business associates, colleagues—can be helpful to you in a number of ways in your transition. Other people can give valuable information and personal feedback so you can:

- create a sharp profile of your passions, strengths, and limitations
- identify good job possibilities that match your career profile
- be knowledgeable about which industries and companies are growing
- interview and create good impressions with people who can hire you

Yet building relationships is easier for some of us than for others. And even if you find it easy, I am sure that there are moments where you think to yourself: *What am I doing? Why isn't this working? Could someone please crack the code on how I can develop relationships, especially at a time when I really need them?*

I had a client who had quit his job a year earlier and was trying to build a business selling computer services. He said, "I really felt like I had a good network and could leverage that into creating a nice business helping companies with these services. I haven't been able to make it work. I thought my network was strong enough to grow this, but it isn't." What makes for strong relationships? How do you build them? You can initiate and build relationships by tapping into the power of behavioral style. We will focus on the basis of all strong relationships.

Building Relationships

Simply put: You build relationships by building trust. What is trust? By most definitions, people are trustworthy if they show characteristics such as the following:

87

- **Congruence.** They are who they say they are; what you see is what you get. They are forthright, without hidden agendas.
- **Unconditional Acceptance.** They value and hold you in high esteem regardless of the circumstances and your behavior. They will accept you for who you are.
- **Steadiness.** They are loyal, deliberate, and committed. You can count on them to do what they say they will do.
- **Being Principled.** You can count on them to get it right, be precise, have their facts correct, and strive for the highest standards in what they do.

Can you do these things equally well? In looking at these characteristics, it becomes clear that specific aspects of trust will be easier for some people than for others. No one will be good at all these. *Being open* and putting all the cards on the table may be extremely natural for the High D profile. While it may be a little in-your-face, it's the hallmark of their style. For the High S profile, being open would be difficult since their style is to be reserved or shy. For the High I, *unconditional acceptance* may come very naturally since they are frequently warm and outgoing. High C's are more inclined to be discerning or even critical. The *consistently steady* approach is natural for the High S profile, but certainly at odds with the mercurial High I. *Being principled and getting the facts straight* are fundamental to the High C profile, but can be a painstaking challenge for others, especially the High I.

The lesson here is that in building relationships, each of us will have our own special strengths and limitations. So recognize and accept that, in yourself and others. Don't waste time blaming others or being ashamed of your own flaws. As you learned in chapter three, the formula for transcending what's difficult is *awareness, acceptance,* and *action.*

Honoring Different Styles

At the opening of the chapter we saw how Raymond felt he was honest because he was so direct. He thought if everything was going so well, why not just go for broke and address the whole hiring issue? His interviewer was overwhelmed by Ray's unvarnished directness and did not respond to him. My guess is that the interviewer wasn't really less honest than Raymond—it's just that his style was different. What Raymond did is exactly what I am hoping you can avoid. He made the rather big assumption that he and the interviewer had the same style.

In your career transition and day-to-day life, your style, strengths, and ways of creating trust will be different from other people's. That doesn't make you good or bad. If you can see and appreciate that, you can build resources and relationships that can help you throughout your life.

Some Last Tips: And What Do You Speak?

Look for the style cues of the people with whom you are communicating. Then try to speak their language—that is, talk in ways they can best understand—and to harmonize when needed. For example, the High D manager I was coaching on interviewing needed me to understand his focus on results and his need to be in control. I was happy to be his "employee" for an hour at a time to help him out. Here are some tips to help you create trust when building relationships.

High D: Cut to the Chase!

High D's speak in terms of results and impact. If your interviewer is High D, get to the bottom line fast. Do let them stay in control. Don't talk too much and when you do talk, be concise. They focus on outcomes and will want the same from you. High D's think in terms of competition and winning, so don't be surprised or feel bullied by this. B-e-h-a-v-i-o-r-a-l style: it's not personal. Be sensitive to their desire to be recognized as winning if it comes up in examples or stories. *Sounds like you won that one!* Similarly, they also like challenge. If you can do so sincerely, convey respect for challenges they have confronted. High D's may more easily respect others who have taken on, survived, or overcome challenges too. Overall, it may be important to convey respect, rather than liking, in making a connection.

High I: Love Me!

High I's speak in terms of connection with others. They highlight the relationships between people and they value harmony—everyone getting along. Let yourself enjoy their warmth and company. Recognize and accept them. Listen with sincere interest. Don't be afraid to give honest compliments, smile when appropriate, and show good humor. Creating good chemistry or a personal connection will be important with the High I. In conversation, they won't be interested in tedious details; however they are likely to be more energized in conversations that focus on creating ideas and concepts than on practical steps.

High S: Order, Order!

High S's language will reflect a focus on stability, making things routine, predictable, and steady. The somewhat shy High S friend or interviewer may not be as forthcoming as others you meet. Stay calm and recognize that this understated style is just that—a behavioral style. It doesn't mean he or she doesn't like you or isn't interested in you. Be deliberate in presenting information. Natural planners, High S's like to see the logic and steps. For example, if you mention a project they appear interested in, don't be afraid to initiate a methodical account of the "what" and "how." Always look for feedback in the process, though. These people can easily get bowled over by others. If their role is to be in the control seat, such as being an interviewer, help them stay in it.

High C: Dot Those I's, Cross Those T's!

Welcome to the world of accuracy, precision, and formality. High C's are the people whose thinking will gravitate to policy and procedures. Specific facts will attract their attention. However, if you use facts, be absolutely correct or skip them. While generally diplomatic and tactful, these people are likely to be very intolerant if you don't say or spell their names correctly. Fulfill commitments 100 percent; that's what creates trust. If they seem critical, it's because they are. But recognize this as being true to their style and don't overreact to it. If they were doing your income taxes, you'd love this about them.

Many people increase the length of their emotional unemployment by alienating people who could help them. Once you learn to understand and accommodate another person's style, you're on your way to a smooth relationship. Knowing about behavioral style also creates neutrality in our own judgments about ourselves and others. *You're not just trying to annoy me about the details, your style is High C and that's what's important to you!* If we allow others to be themselves, they are more likely to be able to make a commitment to us. As you incorporate the concepts and your insights of behavioral style, you'll find that your confidence and power increase. There truly is a science to behavior.

This chapter should have given you an edge in understanding your internal barriers and strengths. It can also help you to develop more effective relationships. Yet your behavioral style is only part of what you need to attend to since, as you saw in chapter three, controlling negative judgments and thinking is not easy. All of us can suffer from a tyranny of the mind, with its fear, worry, and negative evaluations. This mind activity creates a serious strain on our energy, making constructive movement harder. Further, it can keep you from hearing your own inner voice. The next chapter will help you address the challenge of managing your mind. It offers simple and useful approaches to deliberately conditioning your mind for success.

WRITING REFLECTION EXERCISES

1. What aspects of the four behavioral descriptions sound most like you?

2. Which best describe your behavior patterns in your career change?

3. Which of your behavioral strengths do you want to feature in making your career change?

4. What limitations or internal barriers are getting in your way? What do you need to address to increase your effectiveness?

5. What behavioral styles are most difficult for you? Why?

6. Do you see a relationship between your barriers and your behavioral style? If so, what is it?

7. What are the most significant things you learned from this chapter?

8. If you would like an objective assessment and report on your behavioral style, go online to www.back-in-control.com and complete the DISC assessment to receive your own personalized profile report.

CHAPTER FIVE

CONDITION YOUR MIND
FOR SUCCESS

There are mornings when I wake up and everything seems fine. My wife leaves and I start collecting email, checking monster.com, reading through the ads, and thinking about the great opportunity I have with this unexpected change. By noon, I start to cave. The tension has built; my mind gets flooded with the panic. I worry: What if I never find another job? What if my wife gets tired of me complaining and not making any money? What if we can't start our family since we don't have the security? What if she decides our marriage isn't working since I'm not the guy she married—successful, happy, and fun? My head feels like it's going to explode. My confidence goes out the window. I start putting off making calls and just waste time. It becomes a vicious circle.

Abe, mid-forties, describing the process of his career change, which transpired during the last year, salary mid-$50s

M any people I coach are like Abe. Their intentions are great but they struggle with negative, energy-draining mental patterns that can shut down their progress. This chapter is about understanding and using your mind to achieve your highest potential in work and life. It is not simply about putting on a happy face, thinking positive, and lying about how you are feeling to yourself and others. This chapter will focus primarily on your thinking. It will be followed by chapters on taming your emotions and deepening your connection to "that little voice." Since your mind has a mouth-piece in your ear most of the day, it's our best place to start.

The first section will identify key premises about the nature of your mind, its relationship to intuition, and the inner world of emotional unemployment. The second will help you label thought patterns that can get you into trouble. Section three will outline specific practices to get you beyond draining, negative mental habits; to create more energy and confidence; and to make way for your intuition.

THE MIND: YOU ARE MORE THAN YOUR THOUGHTS

Most of us identify who we are by what we think. You want to "have your own mind" and "put your mind to" whatever you want to get done. However, you are *not* what you think. You are more than that.

The mind is based in the world of words, its medium of communication. For most of us, the mind creates a continual, unedited dialogue in our heads about what has happened, what that means, and what will happen. Certain triggers—people, situations or things—set off certain songs or sets of lyrics in our heads. Then the mind is off and running, weaving meaning into events, and telling the stories of what has happened or will happen. Rejected for a job? The "poor me" song kicks in. Friend doesn't call? The "not good enough" lyrics begin. A good interview? The "new job—what will my new life be like?" song starts up.

Overall, the mind is motivated by fear and seeks to protect us. That's why Bolles refers to this side of ourselves as the Safe-Keeping Self. At its best, fear is valuable and can increase your energy and alertness for solving problems. At its worst, the mind will create problems to solve where there were none. The mind will contrive numerous strategies for how to make things better, get it right, and guard your safety. While it endeavors to be practical and logical, the mind is typically busy and undisciplined like a little monkey.

Yet you, your essence, what makes you who you are, is so much more than all this. It can be hard to recognize that, since your intuitive self can easily get drowned out by the chatter of your mind. In career coaching, I tell my clients that our goal is to understand them so they can make their own decisions. I warn them as we work that what seems to be true one day may not be true the next. For example, Sidney says, "I hated my last job! It wasn't me at all." Two sessions later: "I liked the work itself on my last job, but the environment was so toxic that I couldn't do my best." Getting clarity on what is best for you is not a one-shot proposition. It's a process of focusing, getting past your fear-based, protective mind patterns, and conditioning your mind for success.

YOU CAN HARNESS THE POWER OF YOUR MIND

If you need evidence of the power of what your mind is telling you, you can learn from my experiences. Here are two examples.

My Story: "Why Do I Have to Learn All This?"

Several years ago, I decided to apply for the state license in counseling. That involves passing an exam that covers all facets of the field. It generally requires about six months of preparation. Initially there was a rub in it for me since I am a specialist—I work only with adults and focus primarily on career and life planning. Nonetheless, for my license I needed to have a working knowledge of the entire counseling field. I needed to know, for example, why some children are prone to eating crayons and the clinical term that describes this.

To make life easier, I formed a study group of colleagues who were also registered for the exam. We met twice a month and each time I whined and grumbled about having to study *all this stuff I never would use*. Over time, I could see my buddies were working their way through the list of suggested readings much faster than I was, and they seemed to understand what the readings covered better than I did.

Then in my review of materials I came to the sections that discussed which counseling methods worked best for which people. For example, psychoanalysis is helpful for neurotics, but not for those labeled with the diagnosis of Borderline Personality Disorder. Behavioral conditioning is effective for phobias like fear of flying and open spaces, but less so for depression. From all this, I began to see an important pattern. The approaches that helped people

95

change their *thinking* worked for many different types of problems such as depression, anxiety, alcoholism, and even lack of assertiveness. These *cognitive* therapy approaches identify what you are telling yourself and help you change it.

I thought, who better to try this on than myself? I already saw what I was telling myself. Anyone could. *This studying is a waste of time, I hate this. Who wants to know all this?* So, I wrote new things on a card to tell myself. There were phrases like *I am a knowledgeable expert. This will help me be useful to others. I am getting smarter about this information all the time. All learning is good, and I am really enjoying this process.* I put this 3 x 5 card in front of me as I studied in the library. I repeated these sentences a few times a day.

Now at first, I have to tell you, believing these ideas was a big stretch. Yet, it wasn't long before I realized I had started to look forward to the readings. That surprised me a little. It also seemed like the information might be sinking in better. I felt a little smarter to know things about the field even if I wasn't directly using them. And, some of the information really did help. For example, learning more about attention-deficit disorder (ADD) and learning disabilities was valuable in working with my low-achieving clients—even executives—who couldn't quite stay on task with our career work. I could also better see when my clients needed help from other professionals.

The next time my study group met, I was surprised to find I could answer many questions my colleagues had about the material. I felt like the quiz kid! It was amazing. Overall, it was clear that I was learning the information better than I had with my previous approach—whining, just reading through the books, and hoping to memorize everything for the four-hour exam. It was actually funny that I had changed my thinking and dramatically improved my progress without realizing the power of the strategy I had tried. If I can change my own behavior and results, you can too. And yes, I passed the exam.

Jim's Story: "I'm Soooo Tired"

Another example came early in my practice with a client I'll call Jim. Smart, sensitive, and effective, Jim had been promoted to a level of sheer incompetence. He had been a wonderful field manager guiding his customers to grow their businesses through sound advice and friendly counsel. Jim was so effective at this, he was promoted to a prestigious and well-paying position in the corporate offices downtown. Jim's new job was supervising a team of eight representatives out in the field who were doing what he loved and used to do. The new job was overwhelming—not because he wasn't a smart guy, but because it wasn't his passion. He enjoyed being with business owners, knowing everyone in his small town, and helping people.

When Jim came to me, he was depressed and completely exhausted. I asked him what his day was like and how he felt inside. He said it all started the moment his alarm went off. He would feel *sooooo* tired he did not want to get out of bed. As he lumbered his way through his day, he continued to feel drained and talked to himself about it, over and over: *I'm so tired.* As we finished our session, I asked him to do some homework for our next meeting.

Jim's task was to go through his day and count the number of times he said to himself, *I'm so tired.* He came back the next week with his counts. The first day after our session, Jim recorded saying *I'm so tired* to himself a full 140 times. And he had similar totals for the next few days, although after that he stopped counting. He said it was sort of depressing to know how often he said that. Jim said he also had started to feel a little better since he could see what he was doing. In essence, he was hypnotizing himself by saying that over and over.

Our next step was to replace that tiresome phrase with something different and better. He chose what he wanted to be true. It was *I am full of energy.* Jim's task was to say this to himself every time he started to say *I'm so tired* and at least a hundred times a day. He came back for his third session looking brighter and happier, with a little more bounce in his walk. He was feeling and sleeping better although he still found himself slipping into the *I'm so tired* talk. Jim had also come to consider running again, or at least trying to find his running shoes. He began to think that maybe part of his problem was that he didn't get enough exercise and needed to just move more.

In the following sessions he had a wealth of ideas for activities that continued to get him off the dime, where he was stuck and unhappy, and into planning for his next career move. It is a story with a happy ending. We started with his thinking, improved his awareness of what he was doing and his acceptance, and then created new actions to move him closer to his dreams. You can do this too.

RECOGNIZING TROUBLESOME MIND PATTERNS

While your mind may be like a monkey, it is possible to teach a monkey some tricks. Changing your thinking *will* change your life—trust me, that's true. Conditioning your mind for success is simple but not easy. To begin, you must be able to easily spot your dysfunctional thinking patterns.

The following mind patterns are ones I find quite common and often unhelpful. If you engage in any of the following self-talk patterns in your thinking very often, you could be wasting precious time and energy. If you're like most people, you're likely to find more than one pattern that describes your thinking. Labeling your thinking creates the *awareness* needed to *accept* it. Both awareness and acceptance are essential to change. Each self-talk pattern below will be followed by an alternative phrase for you to consider. Let's begin with two very important patterns that are a little broader than the others and then continue with more specific ones.

Small World: *It's All About Me*

How could they have not called me back to schedule my interview? They said they would. I waited and sat by the phone for three days. I'm upset about this. All they have to do is pick up the phone. I'm here!

Basically, fear can make our thinking world pretty small. We see ourselves best and sometimes it's all we can see. In the quote above, there is no understanding that this interviewer has a schedule and competing demands, could be sick, may have a boss who isn't ready to start the interviews, or may have already hired someone else. All our job seeker can see is the interviewer sitting by her phone, not calling him. This small worldview can make you feel stuck and depressed, and convince you there is no opportunity.

Small world thinking is like a Chinese handcuff that fits on your finger. When you try to pull away, the grip tightens. It's maddening, since your instinct is to pull harder and that only makes it worse. The more fearful and self-focused we are, the smaller our world gets. *You need to hire me immediately! I want this career transition over right now! Why aren't my contacts helping me? I'm so mad at them. I hate all this.* Impulsively acting upon what you are thinking only makes it worse.

Authentic creativity is not on the small-world-thinking map. Instead, it creates insidious barriers like infinite lack, jobless paranoia, and career amnesia. That can happen all too easily. You need to see yourself differently to find something different. You must concentrate on expanding your world, especially if you've lost the structure and social contact of a job. Don't let your world shrink so small that all you have is anxious energy. You need to get outside the small, problem-oriented mind to find your success.

Alternative Self-Talk: I care about myself but I also care about others. My world is bigger than my own concerns.

Lack of Identity: *Who Am I?*

I really don't know who I am anymore. I thought I knew myself pretty well, but after losing my job at Anderson, I just feel a little lost.

It's true that our roles can structure our identity and how we see ourselves. When you are going through a change—voluntary, involuntary, or even just growing out of the roles—it does affect your self-image. A key part of the internal transition will be reworking your sense of who you are. Yet this mind pattern can take on a life of its own and become very chaotic. One key way to cope with transition is to remind yourself of what is constant. When you're under personal construction, anchor yourself in your strengths.

Alternative Self-Talk: I have a number of strengths. I may not feel like myself right now but I am working my way through this. I'm okay and I'll be okay.

Also, see the exercises in step four, "Implement Strategy and Monitor Your Progress," below.

Regret: *I Should Have . . .*

I wish I had majored in business instead of psychology. Dad was right, but I just wouldn't listen. I also should have gotten better grades. I should have been studying rather than going out with my friends all the time.

Looking back on the past can be a good idea. However, if you end up reviewing your past mistakes and failures over and over, telling yourself what you *should* have done, you can waste time and kill your spirit. Also, do not let others continually tell you what you should have done. It's not helpful.

Saying "should" to yourself while trying to make decisions can keep you from understanding what you'd really like. I worked with a young man who always believed he should go to medical school. Both parents and all his grandparents were doctors and being a doctor would allow him to make a good living. The first problem was that he didn't want to be a doctor. The second one was that he had no idea what he wanted to do instead. His mind was filled only with "shoulds" and they kept him from hearing his own wisdom. We worked on helping him contact his intuition by first stopping the shoulds. Over time, he was able to awaken to his own aspirations for life.

Alternative Self-Talk: I made the best choices I could at the time. I make my own choices in life.

Negative Self-Talk: *I'm Not Good Enough To . . .*

This is one of the many negative self-talk messages that can emerge and lock your thinking. As we saw in chapter three, many people hold themselves back from doing what they love by thinking they are not good enough. This is often just a fearful reaction. I'm not saying you should not try to get a realistic picture of your talents—do that. For many people, the future is shrouded in fearful self-messages that limit their horizons. It's worth the time it takes to break these old mental habits. There are also a number of negative self-messages that aren't necessarily your self-critic. For example, Jim told himself *I'm so tired* over and over. Another popular one is *I'm too old.* "Diane, I'm too old to go back to school for four years." I think some people become old long before they really are old since they give it a great deal of their focus.

Alternative Self-Talk: Create your own statement to counter the negative statements you are using now. For example, for Jim, it was "I am full of energy."

For more self-talk suggestions, see the section "Ideas for Strengthening Your Identity and Self-Esteem" at the end of the chapter.

Disowning Choice and Responsibility: *If Only . . .*

If only I didn't have to take care of my mother I'd do what I really want to do. If only I didn't have to take care of everyone else I could do what I want. If only I could spend more time doing what matters to me.

The "if only" pattern can protect you from facing your own life challenges, choices, and opportunities. The way you spend your time and the way you think about it *is* your life.

If you find yourself saying "if only" a lot, you may want to ask yourself whether your mind is trying to keep you from making real changes. *If only* can prop up barriers that aren't really obstacles. For example, *I have to wait until my kids finish school before I can take care of myself.* One client of mine said she was putting off her own career to take care of her family. After some lengthy discussion, she decided that it wasn't her family she was concerned about. Beneath it all, she said she was afraid of being unsuccessful at work. With this honest realization, she became free to choose to work on things that really mattered to her, including getting her skills up to date and deciding what type of work situation would fit best. She became happier and her husband and kids were happy to see her doing more for herself.

The *if only* pattern can keep you from learning about who you really are. I found that in writing this book. As invitations and special events came up, I often said to my husband and friends: "If only I didn't have to do my writing, I could do that." They've heard it countless times. Finally, while writing this section, I had to admit: *I love writing this book. I am completely inspired by the prospect of helping you in a way that is positive and important. It is part of my life purpose right now. Many days I can't think of anything I'd rather do.* Saying "If only" kept me from seeing what was true.

Alternative Self-Talk: I am responsible for my life. I am making choices about how I spend my time and energy.

Blaming: *It's All Their Fault!*

> I quit because my boss drove me crazy. He took credit for my work and made my life miserable. He got fired after I left but not before he made my life a mess.
>
> Danny, early thirties, formerly in social work, looking for a new career for four months

I wrote about Danny in chapter two. He quit his job because of his boss. Life is hard and people can be unfair—unwilling or unable to do what is best for us. However, when you are spending most of your time focused on what others are doing, have done, are not doing, or should be doing, you're in a mind pattern that can get the best of you. I've met wonderful people who could only talk about what others could or should do to make their work situation better. Actually, I feel pretty sure I have been one of those people at times! This mind pattern will take your time and energy and while it seems like you are acting in your life, you may be only reacting to others. Maybe it was best for Danny to leave his job. However, when you only blame and react to others, it is hard to do what's best for yourself.

Alternative Self-Talk: I am responsible for my life and choices.

Comparisons: *See What They Have? Why Don't I Get That?*

I look around me and see all my friends doing well. They make more money than I do and they're all on their way to being married and having kids. I can't even get a date for this wedding we're all going to next month. How can they find good work and I'm stuck in limbo? Every time I get a job, something happens.

Comparative thinking gets you nowhere—stuck in the land of jealousy and resentment. Only you can lead the life you're given. You can't live other people's lives and you have your own special path. This way of thinking can only serve to keep your mind busy so you won't have time or energy to move forward.

In my practice, I have seen people who had it all figured out at one point in life and can feel completely lost five years later. I have worked with many fine and talented people who wanted or had a career with Arthur Andersen. I helped college students who wanted the brass ring—entry-level positions that were guaranteed to bless their careers. I coached younger Andersen consultants who worked on engagements that kept them away from home four or five days a week for months at a time. They craved life balance, especially time to date and see friends. Now I see people who need coaching to pick up the pieces after Andersen's demise. We work on what they will do next and how they can present their experiences so the company's tarnished reputation does not work against them.

As the Buddhist teachers say, "Life is impermanent." Everything changes. There is no reason to be jealous or competitive. Be brave and use your strengths to build your own life.

Self-Talk Alternative: I have my own path. I will find what is best for me.

Bitterness: *It Wasn't Supposed to Be Like This!*

> What really galls me is all those dumb people who are just out there mindlessly earning a living with nowhere near the education I have. If there were justice, they'd be in the humiliating position of paying all you people who say you are supposed to be helping me and are not.

This is a snippet of conversation that sometimes lingers in my mind. It was with a woman I'll call Amy. The room seemed to close in as she walked through the office door. Her dress was elegant and perfectly neat; her brief case was very expensive. Her movements were impatient and stiff. She made the appointment because her husband wanted her to get help in finding a job. She explained that she had just finished her master's in business at one of the most prestigious programs in the country. After accumulating a high grade-point average and about $100,000 in tuition expenses, Amy was unable to find a job.

She was resentful about all the people she felt should be helping her and were not. She was bitter about the economic climate, the university's apparent lack of interest in her, and "every moron in the city" who had gotten a job without having her educational pedigree. Beneath this entitled, hard-as-nails exterior was someone trying incredibly hard to take care of herself in the best way she knew. Yet her mind patterns and approach were toxic.

There is at least a little of Amy in all of us. Yet, her pattern of self-talk made it extremely difficult to develop a career and the life she wanted. Eventually, Amy was able to see how her pattern was killing her energy and alienating others. She set her grievances aside long enough to see how she was contributing to her own problems and to find people who could and would help her with support and job leads. Overall, she was able to find her way out of her mind patterns and career dissatisfaction. You can do that too.

Self-Talk Alternative: I accept my circumstances. I respect my feelings. I will use my energy to move forward.

Black and White Thinking: *It's All or Nothing*

I'll either find a perfect job or I will be unhappy forever.

My network will either help me get through this or it will not.

Either computers are my calling or they are not.

I talked with six people who don't have jobs and so I'll never be able to find one either.

Can you hear it? The either/or, all-or-nothing self-talk is limited by definition. There is no consideration that there will be steps to finding what you want, no creating new possibilities from what you do find, and no maximizing conditions so your friends and network can and want to really help you. There is no understanding that the number of jobs in the marketplace now does not reflect what could be out there in a better economic time, or even later in the year. There is no possibility that you might be better at finding a job than those six other people.

Career change means taking risks. It is in the gray shades— between the polarities of black and white—that we can create and shape our own possibilities. We usually need to move out of the confines of all-or-nothing thinking to find the part of the situation we can control. For example, some people will look at a high unemployment rate and conclude they will never be able to find a job. Others will know that there is a hidden job market, and that even part-time work is better than no work.

Alternative Self-Talk: Very few things are black and white. I'm comfortable living in the gray, making opportunities where I can.

Catastrophizing: *What If . . . ?*

Like Abe at the beginning of the chapter, many people get lost in self-talk that starts with "what if?" and takes them on a catastrophic ride. The frenzy of the fear feeds upon itself as your world gets smaller and more fearful. What if:

- I can't get a job?
- I get an offer but the salary is too low?
- my wife leaves me?
- I won't be able to find a job after graduation?

This can easily turn into jobless paranoia, since you are creating stories about what can happen or has happened. Catastrophic thinking can take up such a large share of your thinking that you can end up with career amnesia. Your mind is so busy it becomes difficult to remember what you are doing, what your skills are, and the insights you have gained about your skills, goals, and direction.

Alternative Self-Talk: What if . . . (fill in the blank with a positive idea.) What if transition allowed me to discover something I would have never found in my last job? What if I actually made more money than I made in my last job? What if I found a career that was so much better than the last one I could hardly imagine it?

Impatience: *I Want This Over—Now!*

This self-talk may serve to kick you in the pants and keep you motivated. *Get going, this is taking too long!* However, if you are saying this to yourself all the time, you'll wear yourself out and increase your frustration to a point where you are less productive. Career transition is a process; it's a path with many unexpected turns and opportunities. Continually complaining about how long it is taking will generally not help.

Alternative Self-Talk: I am making progress. This will take the time it takes.

Pessimism: *Nothing Will Ever Make a Difference!*

This negative thinking is like a virus that can infect everything—how you feel, what you say, your energy, and what you do. Psychologist Martin Seligman says depression is caused by believing nothing you do can make a difference. With a poor economy and high technology, it's easy to feel that your efforts are wasted. It seems so easy to send your résumé to a company, yet companies rarely respond to applicants, even to say no. No feedback, no note, and you sent them your life on paper. It's easy to feel that nothing you do will make a difference. This thinking is understandable, yet it will keep you from taking constructive action with what you can control.

Alternative Self-Talk: My focus gives strength. I get what I focus on. I will nurture what's positive. I'll learn from this experience.

Scarcity: *There's Never Enough*

If she gets a job, she'll make more than me. I don't have enough money.

This mental pattern so sharply describes a number of people I know and care about. They see the world as composed of scarcity. They fear that there is not enough time, money, love, happiness, or whatever and can't see what they do have. They approach the job market as "job beggars"—in the words of Richard Bolles—rather than thinking of themselves as a resource for others. I help them land a $150,000-a-year job and they begrudge me a reasonable fee for coaching. They see the world like a pie, and if someone else gets a piece, they believe there is less for them. *If someone else is successful, less for me; if they find great happiness, less for me; or if a friend lands a wonderful job, less for me. If my friend makes more money than me, I'm poor and a loser.* What you begrudge others will be difficult to achieve for yourself. For some reason, it just doesn't seem to work that way. Also, you do get what you focus on.

Alternative Self-Talk: I will focus on the abundance I have in my life. I am thankful for all that I have. I am happy for the success of others.

Many of the self-talk mind patterns result in us focusing on people, places, and things we can't really control: how fast someone answers our email, our bad boss, the political environment, what someone else is making or doing. We may want to set the record straight, make someone responsible for what they did, and get even by not letting go of thinking about how bad they are. The result is that it's all we think about and then, before we know it, we are in the role of a helpless victim in our own lives. It takes our time and energy, and we cannot build the life and career that reflects our true selves.

Millions of people use the Serenity Prayer for daily support. The healing aspect of this tool is to take the focus off what you can't control and work with what you can. Obsessive mind patterns usually place heavy emphasis on things you don't have a chance of changing. It's easy to see why prayer may be a good tool.

God grant me the serenity to accept the things I cannot change, the courage to change the things I can, and the wisdom to know the difference.

ACTION STRATEGIES TO CONDITION YOUR MIND FOR SUCCESS

First, take the time to clear your mind of bad habits of thinking—those that interfere with your growth. Learn to respect yourself. Second, be forewarned that it is hard work, so make a commitment to put in time and effort. Third, it will be very much worth it.

Aaron, mid-forties, partner in a law firm, undergoing a major career and life transition

Here are some tools to free up your thinking and enlarge your world of possibilities. Some of the mind strategies will work more effectively for you than others. Don't engage your inner critic if these don't all work, or work immediately, for you. Don't feel you are failing and will never get it. Immediate success is not the point. The point is that you need to enjoy a process of helping yourself to use your time well, create positive energy, and achieve your potential. The following are ways to change your mental patterns and achieve success. They will help you reprogram your thinking, expand the small world you can find yourself in, and strengthen your self-esteem and sense of identity.

Four Steps to Enhance Your Self-Talk

We've talked about how to reprogram your thinking in a rather general way through Jim's story and mine and many examples. This section will give clear and powerful steps for you to reprogram your own thinking. It can take less than thirty days. There are four key steps.

Step One: Identify the Patterns You Would Like to Change

I would suggest taking a period of at least three days to do this step. This will help you to become more scientific and grounded in your commitment for change and to track your progress in a way that can be eye-opening.

Day One:
1. Throughout your regular day, listen to the patterns of what you say to yourself. Identify the statements that zap your energy and make you feel bad. Write them down as phrases. Try to capture *exactly* what they sound like. Let these voices become very clear.

Days Two – Four:

2. Pick one or two patterns. For example, *I'm tired.* Or, *This will never be different.* I suggest limiting your focus to no more than two patterns at once.

3. Write these one or two troublesome phrases down in a small notebook you can keep with you.

4. Keep a count for three days. Make a mark next to each phrase every time you say it to yourself. You need a baseline of what you are saying. Also jot down the times and places where you are most likely to think this. For example, Jim used to say *I'm so tired* at the start of his day. On the days he didn't say it by 10:00 AM, he was less likely to say it in the afternoon.

5. Create a short profile of the self-talk habit you are about to change. For example, in his first three days counting, Jim said more than a hundred times a day that he was tired. Totals were 140 (Monday), 120 (Tuesday) and 100 (Wednesday). Besides early mornings, he'd say it when he got stressed in meetings. The train ride home was better, as was the evening when he was with his family.

Step Two: Recognize the Purpose These Patterns Served

What can you learn about yourself here? Try your best to answer this but don't get stuck on it if you can't. Everything serves some purpose or we wouldn't do it. You may learn the lesson later. Usually it's our fearful mind just trying to protect us. For example, in my study group, I was afraid I wouldn't pass and would be embarrassed, especially if I studied for six months. Jim's *I'm so tired* protected him from seeing what an incredibly bad fit his job was. That was especially hard to digest since he had moved his family across the country to take the job. If you can't immediately think of the pay-off of your pattern, set an egg timer for five minutes and think about it. Then stop, give it your best guess for the day, and move on. If you'd like, think about it again tomorrow. Meanwhile, rest assured, the purpose of your pattern is that your well-intended Safe-Keeping Self is trying to protect you somehow.

Step Three: Reprogram Patterns with New Talk

You can etch new grooves in your thinking by giving your mind new things to say. In a transition, you must do this when you're not being constructive. This is *exactly* how you condition your mind for success. It is your responsibility and it will make a huge difference in your life.

In your notebook, after each of your problem thought patterns, write out new self-talk statements. Use the alternative self-talk statements I suggested or make ones that suit you better. List all the new statements on one page.

Step Four: Implement a Lasting Strategy and Monitor Your Progress

So, beginning on day five of our sequence, once an hour, on the half hour, repeat each of your new self-talk patterns. Challenge yourself to say them at least ten times a day. Keep a stroke count of how many times you repeat the new patterns. One rule of thumb often used in this type of conditioning is that it takes ten new messages a day for twenty-one days to create a new thought habit. My experiences support this. Be religious about practicing your new patterns—even on the days you don't feel like it. Your unconscious mind can be learning while your fearful conscious mind seems to resist.

Also keep a count of how many times you slide back into the negative patterns you want to change. Have family members help you spot the self-talk in your conversations with them. You'll see progress over time; reward your progress! Create small but real rewards. Send me an email and let me know what you did.

How to Expand Small World Thinking

Small world thinking is the haven for bad thinking. However, you can expand your world by including other people and events. This will help you look beyond your concerns to be more positive and create more opportunities and will support the self-talk reprogramming above. Addressing your thought and self-talk patterns from more than one angle will increase your power to make changes. Here are a range of suggestions to enlarge small world thinking:

- Volunteer to help someone else in their transition; spend thirty to sixty minutes showing them what has worked for you.
- Do a favor for a friend or family member without being asked; expect nothing in return.
- Go to an event in your town that you would not ordinarily attend, such as a movie or talk.
- Change your path; take a different way home tomorrow and observe your surroundings.
- Listen to a different radio or television station than you usually do for twenty minutes.
- Do some volunteer work in your community for a couple of hours a week, helping someone or a cause that really needs additional resources.

Ideas for Strengthening Your Identity and Self-Esteem

How you see yourself *will* influence what you do in your transition as well as your results. To find something better in your work, you must change your view of yourself. But also, as part of the terrain of change, most people will struggle with their self-esteem and sense of identity. While low self-esteem will be a significant barrier, transition can also be a rare opportunity to grow a deeper, richer sense of who you are. Your efforts in this area will be greatly rewarded. This short section has two parts: some additional new self-talk suggestions that I have found very helpful with clients and a short exercise to anchor your most positive sense of self.

More "Self-Talk" Vitamins
- I will learn important lessons during this time.
- I will use my transition to become a better me
- While I may not have a career or job I like, I do like myself.
- I am letting go of who I used to be.
- I have many strengths.

- Transition may have its ups and downs, but I am persistent and hopeful.
- I have talents I must contribute.
- I am loved and valuable.
- I am resilient; I like change and I'll make this work for me.

Pick one or two of these suggestions to add to your mind-conditioning practices. Use them every day. Consider them as vitamins for your mind and spirit.

"What I Like About Me" Exercise

Here is another way to fortify your self-esteem and create that newer and better you. Initially, this exercise will not feel natural for many people, so don't be concerned if it's challenging when you first you try it. Most things that are beneficial for us take us at least a little out of our comfort zone.

Set your egg timer or stopwatch for five minutes. During this time, list any and all the things you like about yourself and your strengths. If you feel stuck and think that you have no strengths, ask a friend to help you. Then identify the seven strengths you like most. Select the ones that resonate most deeply within you as to who you are and who you want to be.

Make a list of these seven strengths with "I am" statements on an index card. For example:

- I am smart
- I am loving
- I am kind
- I am creative
- I am diligent
- I am honest
- I am a person with integrity

Writing each as an "I am" statement will call attention to it more strongly in your mind and heart. Claim your seven signature strengths, ones that reflect who you are and how you want to be seen. Tuck this card into your wallet or portfolio or put it on your computer, somewhere you can see it during the day. This exercise will help you with self-esteem and career amnesia—the barrier where you forget who are and what your strengths are. There is no place for career amnesia in a well-conditioned mind.

Positive information from friends, or even people you don't know well, can also help. I took a Dale Carnegie course years ago. We were divided into small groups and were asked to have each member write down something positive about the others. Each person had an index card we passed around to the other four. I remember this so well. People wrote on my card that I was perceptive, kind, compassionate, and had a warmth that made even strangers feel they had known me for a long time. I carried this card in my wallet for years. It did help anchor my sense of self in chaotic times. I'd also like to think it helped me to have more of these excellent qualities.

Since most people don't know much about mind conditioning, they take their distorted and negative self-talk as the truth. In reality, it's not. You can change your thinking and the results can be magical. Cultivating a high-performance mind does take consistent practice. The strategies you use don't have to be complex. Instead, small steps with one or two new ideas can make a big difference. It's been said that Ben Franklin reviewed his life every evening and made lists and plans of what he thought he could do better. World champion golfer Tiger Woods practices by hitting a thousand golf balls every day. I recommend making a list of strategies you will practice on a daily basis. If you want success and an incredible life, you too will need to condition how you are thinking.

While the mind is a powerful thing that affects your emotional world, during a career transition your feelings deserve their own consideration. The next chapter will help you harness energy from your emotions to move you ahead.

WRITING REFLECTION EXERCISES

1. What self-talk patterns best describe your thinking?

2. Which ones do you want most to change?

3. Which of the action strategies in this chapter did you find most helpful? Why?

4. What will you do differently as a result of reading this chapter?

CHAPTER SIX

LET YOUR EMOTIONS BE YOUR STRENGTH

I didn't expect to be so conflicted about my job search. When I left my job in late January during a great job market and with good experience, I expected that I would catch on quick with another company. But what I found in my mixed emotions was a deep anger about the way I was treated in my job. Even feelings that surfaced, of all places and times, on my honeymoon.

Frank, late thirties, unemployed six months after working as a retail floor manager, has been looking for a new position for three months

Even though there are hundreds of books on how to choose your next career, create a good résumé, and master the employment interview, very few books have focused on the emotional world of people in career transition. As a consequence, many people are ill-prepared for the emotional roller coaster that is often very much a part of the journey. Even those familiar with Kubler-Ross's stages of grieving presented in chapter one may be perplexed by their own complex reactions. In the example above, Frank was happy to leave his job and left it voluntarily. He had planned his wedding for months. So why did these angry feelings surface during his honeymoon?

Emotions are a tremendous source of energy and strength when we are able to understand and manage them. Yet they can become toxic when they are not understood. This chapter will help you learn more about the emotional world you may visit in career transition—including some less than obvious reasons for your feelings running the gamut. It will then give you tools to use that powerful emotional energy to improve your ability to live, love, and find your way through career changes.

WHAT'S IT LIKE? THE DAILY EMOTIONAL WORLD OF TRANSITION

In chapter one, Kubler-Ross's framework helped us identify the key reactions of anger and depression. We also discussed earlier the emotional storms and vertigo that are triggered by challenging circumstances. And fear is a reaction that continually resurfaced as we looked at the barriers people face and how to condition your mind for being successful in transition. Here are more voices to help you understand the emotional texture of the daily lives of others in transition. The question that prompted these responses was: *How do you feel day-to-day in your transition?*

My feelings range through frustration, boredom, and embarrassment. The job search is frustrating; we've already talked about that. Boredom, because it feels like I have too much time on my hands. Embarrassed to see some of my neighbors during the day.

Michael, late thirties, consultant, financial services industry, unemployed two months, searching for a new career for one month

I have had some strange juxtapositions of feelings that never occurred before. On the treadmill, while I was working out yesterday, I first felt elated from a song and then I started crying—I can't really explain that one. But in general I feel very hopeful and much clearer about myself and the world I live in.

Aaron, mid-forties, partner in a law firm, undergoing a major career and life transition

My feelings seem to swing so much it makes me feel neurotic sometimes. Mostly I've been feeling more positive lately, but still get depressed. I can get very stressed about not doing good enough work on my transition. I stay down until I feel

I've done something particularly well. Then my spirits start to rise again.

Erin, early forties, currently a public relations executive for a major municipal public organization, salary $50,000

I feel high and low. I am excited about the prospect of change. I am sad the old life has ended. I am sad the whole department has dissolved. The last three weeks of my work were shredded, trashed, and destroyed. I wonder, what was the meaning of all the work?

Maggie, mid-fifties, laid off one month ago from her position of six years as a communications specialist, seeking a career change

On a typical day in my transition, I'd have incredible fear—my heart would pound and I would feel confused and aimless. Or, I would feel preoccupied and driven by ditsy things like what my neighbors were doing. I could be completely absorbed with the maintenance of my indoor plants or what was happening on the street outside my house. The time would just whisk by. What happened to my day? How could I be so happy doing nothing? Especially since I was completely lost?!

Mary, late forties, reflecting on a transition and loss earlier in her life

A typical day is a day at work knowing that I am in transition—it gives me a secret feeling of freedom! I won't be here forever! And that makes it easier to accept some of the circumstances and get through the day. Other times I feel let down—where will I go? What will I do? Will I make enough money? Then I step back and continue doing the small steps to move on. I can't think of big change as "all at once" so I just focus on the small change that will eventually bring about greater change. In general I have a feeling of confidence that nothing but good can come from this process.

Amanda, late fifties, customer services manager, salary $55,000, considering a career change

WHY YOUR EMOTIONS MAY RUN THE GAMUT IN TRANSITION

Your feelings don't have to make practical or logical sense. They just are what they are. And what they are is an essential part of what makes you uniquely who you are. What you do about how you feel is, of course, another story. My first job as a counselor was working with recovering drug addicts and alcoholics. Many of them were young, smart, and wonderful people who had unfortunately learned dysfunctional and even dangerous behavior patterns to manage their emotions. It made me appreciate the power of our feelings as well as the habits we can get stuck in while trying to avoid them. Facing and using our feelings to learn is the best approach. However, it's easier to accept and step out of them when we understand them.

This section will help you understand some of the less obvious reasons for your feelings in transition and to put them into perspective. Your ability to feel your emotions is the basis of power behind all passion in life and work. I sometimes tell my clients who are sad, angry, or upset, "It's okay." "You're entitled to your feelings." "You're alive and you can feel."

The Ping-Pong Ball Effect

Like Frank at the beginning of the chapter, you may have feelings that are a complete surprise. No one dreams of feeling deeply angry on his honeymoon about a job he left voluntarily months earlier. Yet sometimes it is because you feel safe or because your more pressing concerns have subsided that some of your deeper emotions can surface. We push down feelings when they are too painful.

I call this the Ping-Pong Ball Effect. Keeping down your emotions is like trying to keep a ping-pong ball under water in a glass. It's possible, but requires steady concentration. Then when you are safe or if you need to put your concentration on other things, it is like taking your finger off the ball. It pops up, in the same way that the feelings suddenly appear. If emotions like sadness or anger suddenly emerge, it could be a sign that you are now ready to deal with them, even if it's not easy.

You May Suffer from Emotional Unemployment

If you feel out of sorts, vulnerable, and more emotionally reactive, you may just need emotional employment. You may feel like you have lost a part of yourself without work as a focus, like a balloon that has lost its air. Work allowed you to connect with who you are. Of course, your identity is probably more than what you do at work. However, if your work roles allowed you to connect squarely with your highest intuitive purpose, you can feel empty and insecure without it.

Having found meaningful work once is often an asset in finding or creating it again. Similarly, people who have long and good marriages may be most likely to find long and good second marriages. The ability to make a commitment is positive and is evidence you'll be able to do it again.

You Have Accumulated Stress

The effect of losses and stress can be both profound and subtle at the same time. I once worked with a young woman, Kay. The software firm where she worked had referred her to me for career planning, to help her decide what she really wanted to do. She was a valuable employee to them but she was unhappy and had started to withdraw at work. She was more frequently late and talked less and less to her co-workers. Kay said nothing was really very interesting to her right now or made her feel that satisfied.

She filled me in on her recent history. A project Kay worked on for a year had recently ended. She loved the work team, but two of the people she liked most had left the company. This was her third new boss in a year. Her brother was called into active duty in the Middle East. She had recently gotten married and moved into their new apartment. The wedding was nice, but she felt bad her father wasn't able to be part of it. Over the last few months, his Alzheimer's had become much worse. His doctor and the nursing home staff didn't think he should go out for the event.

It's like a photograph developing. There is a moment when suddenly the picture takes shape. The cumulative pattern of Kay's stresses in the last year was rather profound. By the end of our discussion, that picture became clear for her as well as for me. I know that changes in work and life happen all the time, but you must still be aware that major events cause stress. Good news, bad news, and shifts like moving all require our psychic energy. Over time, Kay's personal and work losses and gains changed her situation dramatically. Her sense of disinterest and unhappiness was the result of being fatigued from managing these stresses. Yet Kay couldn't acknowledge being tired. She thought she should feel lucky since she still had a job, her brother was okay, her father was alive and being well cared for, and she was happily married. Once she recognized the cost of stress, she began to figure out ways to rejuvenate, and Kay, a good planner, did just that.

Your Self-Esteem Is in Tatters

Some work situations can leave you feeling thin-skinned and fragile. You may begin to second-guess yourself a lot. For example, you may have an abusive boss who makes you feel chronically stupid, or co-workers who use you as a scapegoat. All too common is the work situation where you feel absolutely no sense of control over your destiny for weeks and months on end. Your confidence wears away from being unable to master your surroundings and life. You can't plan, don't know what will happen, and always are wondering about next week.

Jack, a neighbor of mine, worked for a company that was going through an endless merger situation. He thought his position would be eliminated. If that happened, Jack would get an incredibly good buy-out package, including months of severance pay. He was miserable but stayed and stayed at the company hoping to be let go. The company was chaotic and doing poorly. For months, Jack did work he felt had no real purpose. He was surrounded by many backbiting, scared people and, like them, he became obsessed with the merger details.

Jack's mind was constantly filled with a sea of details about things he could not control: stock prices, who said what, and the state of the economy. He forgot what he was good at and how to take control of his life, and the tension came out in his relationship with his fiancée. Once Jack got his severance package, he left. It took him a whole year to get back his sense of emotional balance. He might have been better off finding a new position in a steadier company than staying in the war zone as long as he did. Of course, hindsight is 20/20. It was a hard decision to stay or leave, and unfortunately both had a high cost.

Misery Has Become Your Friend

People are often surprised to find themselves unhappy after leaving a position that made them miserable. This is quite common. For example, I had a client once who had been at a company where his talents went unrecognized for over ten years. Sean's boss never gave him credit for anything. Sean worked to create a comfortable savings and then left the company. His plan was to take some time off to find something better. In two weeks, he was miserable and could not understand why. He came for counseling after his friends told him they didn't want to hear about it anymore. He needed to do something.

I believe Sean had become attached to his misery. He was so used to thinking, *I'm a miserable guy, I hate my job and boss,* that misery became a part of his emotional and thinking patterns. Sean needed time and coaching to change. That was not easy, since his misery had become predictable. In misery, Sean knew what would happen even if he didn't like it. He began to shift away from misery by dealing with the feelings underneath the protective pattern. For Sean, that meant uncovering a deep sense of anger and shame the job had caused. He did deal with his feelings, and eventually broke free of his pattern using some of the methods in the section, "How to Deal with Your Emotions in Transition," later in this chapter. Sean was able to channel his energy into creating the life he deserved.

Your Earlier Losses Were Triggered

It is not uncommon for career losses to trigger the emotions from past unresolved or even resolved losses. This could include the death of a friend, family member, or even a pet. Maybe you never cried or felt sad when a close friend died. In transition, we can find ourselves attempting to finish other unfinished business, even from losses that occurred years or decades ago. Don't be alarmed; it can and does happen.

Even if you were able to complete your grieving process in the past, current losses may still remind you of earlier ones. This can be positive if you remember that you were able to get through difficult feelings before and you will do it again. For example, I had one client who was put in outplacement after his job was eliminated. In our first session, he began telling me about what it was like when his mother died. He said that thinking about his mother gave him a sense of her presence. And with that, he felt an assurance that he would get through this okay too.

You Are a Square Peg Leaving a Round Hole

Some people in transition feel euphoria and joy that is beyond their comprehension. If you were in a job that didn't need your strengths, you may have felt like a square peg in a round hole at work. An example is an extroverted individual hired to do quality analysis in a software firm. She would find it difficult to sit silently at a computer screen looking for subtle flaws in data programs. After leaving an ill-fitting position, you need time to unfold those parts you've had to fold in to fit into the work hole. You may need time to get to know these parts of yourself again before you can move forward. This can bring on a range of feelings, including confusion, happiness, and fulfillment.

Watching people go through such a reclaiming process is fascinating. Some can try new skills like writing or public speaking; others discover a curiosity for learning what had become deadened in their previous jobs, and it comes alive. Reclaiming your talents can make you feel stronger and steadier.

Anniversary Effects Have Intensified Your Reactions

Our emotional responses can be hard-wired by events we may not be conscious of moment-to-moment. In therapy they are called anniversary effects, and once brought to your conscious mind, are usually easier to deal with. For example, you may find yourself feeling sad, depressed, or insecure around the same time of the year, or on the same day, when you experienced traumas such as the death of a family member or friend, or even a car accident. Part of you remembers and is mourning. An anniversary doesn't have to throw you into a major depression, but it can bring a tide of emotions that you work through again. Anniversary effects can intensify the emotional transition of your career changes.

You've Run Out of Pictures

Our visions, goals, and expectations about life shape our emotional lives and approach to career planning. I once worked with a very pleasant woman called Bella who was just turning thirty-six. Married with two children, Bella was gainfully employed as an accountant. She said recently she had absolutely no idea what she wanted to do with the rest of her life. Her home and job were relatively satisfying, but in the last few months she had begun to feel completely lost. It seemed interesting that she felt as lost as she did, and so suddenly. People grow and change across time and yet this felt a little different.

I tried to understand how Bella had built her career and life and what her dreams were. Curiously, she didn't have any dreams or pictures for after this year. Most people have some visions about themselves growing older, becoming a grandmother, sitting in the park—pictures about later, even if they are not goals. Bella did not. I asked her more about her background and parents. Her father was living in another city and was involved with his other family. "Other?" He remarried many years ago. "And your mother?" Pause. Her mother was dead.

"I'm sorry. When did she pass away?"

Pleasant nod from Bella. "I was eight years old."

"How old was your mother?"

"She was thirty-six."

The insight began to take form. Bella was turning thirty-six. In this and later sessions, it became clear to both of us that this little girl who lost her mother had created an emotional picture of life that didn't include living after age thirty-six. I'm not talking about a conscious, logical picture. Deep inside, Bella had no internal picture of how her life would go. She felt truly lost. With time, Bella saw how her mother's death had shaped her beliefs and emotional responses. Through honoring her emotions, Bella also became free to plan her own life.

You can find yourself out of pictures in other situations, such as when you have set a big goal and achieved it. Maybe you are an athlete and trained years for a certain level of performance, or you wanted to finish law school and become a partner in a firm. Your success can bring confusion, frustration, and anxiety.

Grieving Can Take Many Forms

The work of grieving losses can take time and may have different forms across time. Losing a job can be like a death. My best friend's father recently died and her experience with grief has similarities to job loss. At first she thought she was over all her grieving since she knew her father was dying for months. Lately that's shifted. Some days, she's okay. Other days, she has a dull sadness that doesn't leave. Some days, her grief feels like sharp emotional pieces. She has very sad spells that are like passing a kidney stone—miserable beyond comprehension. But when it's over, she says she feels okay and sometimes good. The feelings come in waves. Getting the emotions out is so important. It helps you feel strong again. If you have experienced many job shifts, the process does seem to get easier.

How to Deal with Your Emotions in Transition

Throughout this book, we've talked about a number of people and situations when dealing with feelings will be the answer to mastering a transition. There was P. J., the wonderful but angry, former pharmaceutical executive; Amy, our unemployed MBA; Bart, the recovering drug addict and emergency room doctor; Sean above; and many others. But just how do you deal with feelings? How does anyone turn these messy, irrational impulses that flood our soul and minds into our strengths? And you can add my name to the list, because since I started this project of documenting how to navigate transition, I seem to have had to experience all the crazy ambiguity, euphoria, and wrenching rejection that I am writing about!

You can use your emotions to create the strength you need, I promise. The following eight sections will give ideas and, I hope, inspiration to do this.

Make Time for Your Feelings

In transition, you must be realistic about the emotional price you may need to pay at times to get through. If you lost your position unexpectedly, or even if you planned it, you may want to go easy on yourself for a short period. Some people take a brief vacation. If you only schedule the time you need to accomplish specific tasks, your emotions can surface to sabotage you until you've given them the attention they need.

Talk, Rave, and Cry

Sharing your feelings is so important. For example, if you felt like a victim in your job, you might develop a sense of shame that could undermine your self-esteem unless you confront those feelings. Facing the feelings will help you to be more realistic about what is happening. In earlier chapters, we saw others—like P. J. and Amy—who fought their sense of shame by fighting with everyone else. Once I worked with a smart, capable, impressive guy named Paul, who was let go from his directorship at a software company due to a restructuring. His job search of fifteen months had many ups and downs. There were times when it looked like he'd landed a position and his life was moving along happily ever after (if there is such a thing). And then the position he'd applied for would close, or the division he was working for would be spun off.

In one situation, he had an incredible day of interviews with a company. He liked the people, they liked him, and he was a very good fit for the position. Paul was told he was one of two candidates for the job. Having done a great deal of networking with his colleagues, Paul knew who else was being considered for the position; it was actually a friend. Two days after his day of interviews, Paul got a call from his friend. He had gotten another offer he was going to take. Paul was delighted. With his friend out of the picture, he waited for the phone to ring with an offer from the company. Eventually they did call and said they had made a decision. They ended up promoting an internal candidate for the position—a third person Paul didn't even know was in the running.

In time, the mind can understand all this. But initially, the heart sinks and can get stuck in sadness. When at home, Paul refused to do anything more constructive than to play solitaire on his computer for almost a week; his girlfriend was worried. Then when he finally came in for his next session after the bad news, Paul sobbed his way through it, ranting loudly about the injustices in his life. He was 100 percent correct. His life was unfair. In reality, he was a victim in the truest sense. This situation wasn't his fault and he was powerless in some key ways. Confronting and honoring this reality allowed him to have compassion for himself and pull together his resources to move on. He didn't need to wear a shroud of shame. He could learn from this somehow and become an even stronger and more sensitive leader in life and work. Everyone needs safe places to talk, rave, and cry their way through their feelings.

Have a Bad Day

Sometimes you need to let yourself have a bad day. Have a day when your only goal is not to struggle to transform your feelings into anything better than they are. You might lie on your bed or the couch. Take a recess like when you were a child at school. Don't worry about anything. Let yourself feel bad or any way you want. Turn off your phone and let the world take care of itself without you. Skip the news. Stay in your pajamas. Eat chocolate.

Get Out That Poison Pen

Journaling helps me to sort through my doubts, concerns, beliefs, and emotions and narrow my thinking to what is really important.

Ellen, fifty-eight, unemployed for ten months to make a career change from the financial investment area

Writing out your grievances is a powerful antidote to misery and confusion. A body of research supports the use of journal writing to improve your ability to cope with stress and physical pain, as well as get better results in a job search. I recommend that people read Julia Cameron's book *The Artist's Way* and follow her suggestions on writing "morning pages." These are three hand-written pages done first thing in the morning. They allow you to get the emotions entwined in your fearful thinking out of your head and onto paper. Let the mind have its say and then get on with your life. I have found keeping a journal to be a good way to tap into my intuition. Buy yourself one of those nice empty books you can find in most bookstores and honor it with your thoughts on a regular basis. I'll give you more ideas on writing in the next chapter.

Exercise Your Body

I ask that all my clients in transition create an exercise regime. Research shows that for treating clinical depression, for example, exercise can be as effective as psychotherapy. It's hard to work on transition if you don't tend to your body in this way, since it's something that can quickly make a significant difference. Exercise can help you develop strength, energy, and emotional calm. If you feel as if you can't control your life, you'll feel better if you can control your body. Get strong, run like a racehorse, punch a bag, shoot the basketball, or take a walk outside. All this will help you let your emotions contribute to your psychological as well as physical strength.

I have gone through periods of time when I hated to exercise. Hated it! I had to work very hard to get out of these slumps. One thing that works well for me and my clients is to make *extremely small* goals and then check them off when done. For many of us, checking things off can bring great satisfaction. I love it. For example, instead of starting with a goal of jogging two miles, decide that you will find your running shoes. I also think *going* to the gym is good, even if you don't run or work out. Part of life is just showing up—maybe it's just to take a sauna, get a massage, or see your pals. Being in the gym will get you closer to doing more. I started back exercising this last time by doing the stationary bicycle only five minutes a day. Feeling guilty never worked. I've tried that many times. What will work is to take small steps.

Distract the Baby

We've all seen it. The baby is hopelessly upset—she's screaming and crying and won't stop. We force a smile and ask in a loud, happy voice, "Wanna see the puppy? Wanna go outside and play?" Miraculously, she shifts her attention and forgets—at least for the moment—what she was upset about. Crying stopped, she smiles. This is one thing we do for children that we need to remember to do for ourselves sometimes. Distract ourselves. You can get an emotional reprieve by shifting away from the hurts, sadness, or rage for a brief time. You'll avoid wearing yourself out with your feelings and get some perspective. *Nap? Cookie? Go outside?* Scoop up that nice baby within yourself and give her a treat. *Coffee with friends? Window shopping?* These reprieves can allow you to come back to your emotions with a better frame of mind. You can learn from your emotions, but don't let them wear you out.

Consider Meditation

A friend of mine married a widower with three teenage children. He is a biologist whose first wife died suddenly. When the children were very young, the family went to the beach. While there, the young mother had a heart attack and died in front of all of them. Incredibly curious, I asked my friend how her new husband had coped with something as tragic as that. She said he credits his meditation practice. He had never meditated in his life, but someone at his church mentioned it to him, and he decided to try it. When the children went to bed he would do his practice. Meditation gave him a way of separating himself from his unbearable pain. When I think of meditation, I have this moving image of a young father alone with three young kids, bravely looking for a way to face life and find solace from the unthinkable. While it takes a little discipline, meditation can be a very powerful tool. It can help you get past emotional storms in your career transition. I'll tell you how to do it in the next chapter.

Find the Lesson

Looking at your emotions can lead to valuable lessons. They can tell you a story about who you are and what's important to you. Sometimes just knowing that there are lessons to learn from your emotions is very helpful.

I remember working with a very smart young woman who sold software solutions products. Lisa had moved to Chicago from the West Coast. Her family was a pillar of their community. Lisa had been in every sport in high school and had gotten excellent grades in both high school and college. However, six months into her first job, her new boss treated her as if she were stupid. Her work was very stressful since her company's products weren't that competitive, and Lisa was having a terrible time managing her over-sized customer territory. It looked like she might not make it through her probation period and would be fired. The rest of her team placed bets on how long she'd be around. Nothing about Lisa's experiences in life prepared her for being a loser.

During Lisa's first session I said, "I don't understand how this situation came to be what it is or how you will get out of it. But I do know we'll work on it together and figure out what there is to learn from it." Her whole life was in shambles, but she was smart and latched onto the idea that she could find insights that could help her later. Through absorbing the concepts in this book, journaling, and lots of discussion, Lisa realized how fortunate she had been in her life; how her teammates might mistrust her intentions because of her behavioral style; how to spot an insecure manager; how to evaluate a company before taking an offer; and how to be less judgmental of other people who weren't as naturally talented as she was. In her more positive learning mode, she made contact with a former classmate who worked for a better company, and within two months she had a new job. Lisa became wiser, humbler, and better for all of this. We can't control others but we can control what we learn from life and where we let it bring us. Her emotional life became an excellent school for her.

Reflections on Fear: Find the Love

I acknowledge it. I say I am so afraid. I feel it—dry mouth, wet palms, tears, nausea, headache, stomachache. I imagine the worst. But I stop short of calling myself bad names—fool, idiot, failure, burden—all the no-no's. For at the end of fear is a decision: depression or courage? Depression is not appealing when one has to get on with life. Courage is. So, I say, yes I'm scared, you bet I am. And keep telling myself until I hate the sound of it. Till I can see and remember how well and kindly I am cared for.

Julie, forty-eight, former project manager for a research and development firm, describing her transition after losing her job over seven months ago

We've talked a great deal about the fearful mind—emotions that get stuck in protective mind patterns—and the importance of your intuition. The last suggestion I have for letting your emotions be your strength in transition and life is this: Every challenge we face offers us the option of going to fear and fear-based thinking, or opening our hearts to feel love and a world of possibility. Every choice point has that duality. If you lose your job, you can hate the company, the economy, your parents, or whomever. Or you can love the options you now have and the freedom you could feel. Living in fear limits not only your possibilities but also the love you can feel in these moments that comprise your life.

When I first had the idea for this book, three publishers were very interested. I thought one would take it, I'd finish writing the manuscript, and it would be smooth sailing into the bookstores within months. Then, within one summer week, one by one, each said "no thanks." I was devastated and cried for days. I cancelled everything except my coaching clients. I felt like a wounded animal and wanted to hide until I could find some protective skin. My writing project had allowed me to connect with a message I believed people needed to hear—to listen to each other and to have faith and strength facing adversity. But life wasn't going to be that simple for me. I believe I needed to feel and more intimately learn the lessons I wanted to teach. I needed to stand back, connect with my purpose, and emerge from my fear-based thinking. I needed to trust—myself, the universe, and a power greater than myself—and then do my part. I think that's what we all need to do, in the best ways we can.

WRITING REFLECTION EXERCISES

1. Describe your own emotions. How do you feel day-to-day in your transition?

2. Could you relate to any of the less than obvious reasons for your emotions during transitions? If yes, which of these patterns seemed most like yours? How so?

3. How do you make your emotions your strength? What ideas, if any, did you learn from the suggestions above? Do you use other strategies to deal with your feelings? If so, describe these.

4. Preparation: Get some blank writing paper and a stopwatch or egg timer. Sit in a place you can relax. For example, a coffee shop, your home, or a library. For twenty minutes each day, write whatever comes to your mind on the paper. Don't critique yourself. Be honest. This will help you know your own story as well as release your emotions. More on journaling in the next chapter.

CHAPTER SEVEN

CULTIVATE INTUITIVE GUIDANCE

TURN UP THE VOLUME ON THE LITTLE VOICE

I'm stuck with this career stuff. I know I need to listen to my little voice and I try. Usually there's nothing there—like the volume is on mute. After a while I start thinking about food. What can I eat? What's in the kitchen? Is it too early to eat again? My little voice seems to be hungry a lot and is sorta whiny.

Gena, late thirties, financial services professional who was laid off twice in two years, has been looking for a new position for twelve months

About ten years after I started my coaching and counseling practice, I became aware of a subtle pattern in the development of my successful clients. Something similar happened to many people who met very different goals in different ways. This included those who discovered their calling, landed jobs they really wanted, succeeded in leading their companies or departments in the most fair and brilliant ways, handled tough interpersonal work situations for successful outcomes, and were true to themselves in profound ways. Things clicked for them; they did well or found what they wanted, often after being in some pretty tough spots.

I am not saying these people didn't work hard on all the lessons we've talked about—like tapping into the power of their behavioral style and knowing their own story. They did the preparation. But there was something more. When I began to try to think about what had happened, I could easily create a picture of each person sitting across from me. These were people I knew and cared about. But, it wasn't what they looked like or the fact that I cared that figured into this. The pattern came from what it felt like to be in this picture as they moved into their triumph.

The pattern was that each of these people had a shift of some type before meeting their goal. Things were different for them after this shift. When my realization began to emerge, I certainly had no way of understanding it. But I was curious. I thought if my clients who were successful had this—whatever it was—maybe I could teach it to others. For example, it could be very useful to people like Gena, above, and Francis, the accounting executive from chapter three, who couldn't seem to make much progress.

With time and research, I did learn more about what had happened with these clients. Basically, they plugged deeply into their intuition for guidance. There are important things you need to know about how and why that worked—why I could feel it physically sitting across from them, and how *you* could feel that from within yourself too. That's what this chapter is about.

THE INTUITIVELY GUIDED

We've talked a great deal about what it means to be dominated by the mind, or Safe-Keeping Self, and barriers that can arise from that. We have yet to create a clear picture of those who show a healthy intuitive side.

Here's what the successful clients mentioned above had in common: they were humble yet strong, anchored in their knowledge of who they were, and they acted like learners rather than know-it-alls. They weren't caught up in destructive thought patterns and feelings. They felt their passion and encouraged others to do so too. They did not begrudge others their success and enjoyed their own. There was a generosity and compassion in their minds and hearts. They were not filled with resentment. Their energy came from a deep passion to be more of who they were and to contribute to the highest good, while living well and providing for their families.

These aren't the kind of people who never have sadness or pain. When they do, they honor it, use it to grow, and move on. I see these people being internally guided and intuitively connected. Their little voice is usually their intuition rather than their nagging, fearful minds, or at least they have skill in figuring out the difference. Getting to this level of intuition is simple but not always easy.

A good example of someone who made the journey is Lisa, from chapter six. When I first met her, her situation was pretty difficult. She was depressed, had gained ten pounds in six months, and cried every night after work. (I've met many people with emotional unemployment who cry almost every night.) She had become alienated from her team, was a scapegoat for her boss, and was in a quandary about how to proceed. There was an adult "launching issue" like I described in chapter one, which stemmed from the fact that our first real job is often so important. It results in questions like: *Can I really make it in the adult world? Can I be independent, make a living, and be successful?* For Lisa, it also included these thoughts: *Gee! I did so well in college! Everyone thought I'd be running corporate America by age thirty-eight, and here I am feeling like a loser—waiting to get fired. And I'm fat!* (For some women and even men, that last part would be the worst.) There was subtle pressure from her parents, who wanted Lisa to do well for herself and—the truth be told—to reflect well on them. Even the best parents can have those concerns. So how did she tap into her intuitive intelligence and what does that feel like? I'll tell you more about that through Lisa's story and some others.

SIGNS OF INTUITIVE INTELLIGENCE

Most of us float in and out of our intuitive side throughout the day. Yet the intelligence of our intuition is there all the time—that little voice is talking. The issue is how much we can hear it through the chatter of our minds. The following sections describe some qualities of being connected to your intuition.

Alertness to Hunches and Signals

You hear the signals of your sixth sense—they might occur as flashes of insight. For example, when Lisa contacted the friend who told her about a better job, it was just a hunch to make the call. The timing was uncanny since the position had just opened. In transition, your intuition is often felt in knowing what is right for you, moment to moment as well as in making big decisions. Maybe you can't describe exactly what is right but you certainly know if you are close to it. It is similar to seeing for the first time someone you know you could love forever.

Your hunches can also signal what not to do. I'll never forget a job I almost took before I started my practice. Everything seemed fine. It was a logical move for me to make. It met all my requirements for an ideal job. Just before taking the offer, the human resources manager took me to the desk where I would sit. It was reasonably attractive, but suddenly all my internal alarms went off. Inside, a firm voice shouted: *"Absolutely No Way!"* I've heard people say similar things about selecting a new house or apartment. Looking back, I can see that taking that job would have been a huge mistake.

Awareness of Positive Possibilities

When Lisa first came to me for coaching, she was doing "what if" thinking. She asked me, "What if I can never do a good job for my boss? What if I managed to do a good job, but he could never see it? What if I just keep gaining weight? What if this was the only job I could ever get in Chicago? What if my family starts thinking I am going to be a loser?" As her awareness grew about what a difficult mind pattern she was in, she reconnected with the part of her that knew she was very smart and could figure things out. She began to see positive possibilities. What does it feel like to experience such a reconnection?

With the sense of positive possibilities, everything informs you—movies, books, and people all have something to teach you that is, or could be, relevant. The newspaper has a story about a company that is expanding; you know someone who works there—maybe that's an option for yourself or someone else. Lisa saw a newspaper article about a company where her friend worked and she called to congratulate her on their company's success. Actually, her own job search wasn't even her first thought in this but it brought that possibility.

Sense of Effortlessness

What is difficult while your mind is struggling can be easy when you engage your intuitive side. Your concentration becomes present-oriented and focused. You enjoy what you are doing and can lose the sense of time.

Many people know that when Phil Jackson coached the Chicago Bulls during their heyday, he trained his team in both mental and physical skills. A self-described Zen Christian, Jackson cultivated the higher performance of his players by having them focus their attention on being in the present moment. I had the great pleasure of being in an audience that witnessed one of the most awesome shots in basketball history. It was during one of the play-off games and went like this.

Michael Jordan's legs launched him into the air. His leap propelled him above the shiny, hardwood floor, up, and up, and up, seeming to defy gravity. As thousands of us watched in awe, the basketball rolled through his hands, passing from one to the other in mid air, to delicately tilt off the last hand and go purposefully down into the hoop. Yes, it went gently *down* through the hoop. Time briefly stood still; the entire stadium sat stunned in silence and then broke into a screaming frenzy. It was a moment of beauty and flawless perfection, concentration to surpass all concentration, and a resulting action that was as effortless and natural as it was incredible. Jordan had made what appeared, even to jaded veteran observers, to be an impossible shot in a pressured situation. And proved, of course, that he actually can fly!

While you can't always be in a zone "like Mike," you can definitely appreciate the effortlessness that comes with being fully present and acting upon your instincts. If your concentration and work are effortless and enjoyable, that's a sign you're connecting with your intuitive energy.

Ability to Tolerate Uncertainty

When you draw on the intuitive side, you're able to understand and maybe even relish the lack of organization that change can bring. You stop trying to put all your ducks in a row. Career change, getting laid off or fired, or hating what you currently do may not be fun. When you tolerate the uncertainty, things get better faster. Uncertainty brings us back to the idea of finding out what we can control and what we can't, then doing what we can and leaving the rest alone. And, yes, that's how we get back in control.

When Lisa stopped trying to create order and certainty where there was none, her situation got better. She couldn't fix Ben (her bad boss), make the services she sold more competitive, or know immediately what her next career move would be. Instead, her response was to get curious about what was happening, to see what she could learn.

Tolerating ambiguity and taking that learning attitude allowed Lisa to create a bigger picture of what was happening. It occurred to her that since Sharon—her previous manager—was a long-time friend, maybe her boss felt threatened. Sharon was a talented woman who had been hired away by a competitor. In the short-term, Lisa could see how difficult it must have been for Ben to take over a sinking ship. It certainly didn't justify Ben's attitude toward her, but she no longer felt so bad about how he had behaved. She stopped feeling so defensive and started to treat him with a little compassion, or at least didn't let everything he did bother her so much. Her day-to-day stress was lower as the friction between them diminished. She began to sleep better, which increased her coping skills. When Lisa's boss started to treat her with more respect, her team followed suit. She relaxed a little and learned how she had contributed to their reactions. For one thing, while she was sad at home and with me, in her fearful work environment, she had adapted a High D style. That had earned her the reputation of being bossy and controlling.

Sense of Well-Being, Even Joy

While the feelings associated with the mind are fear and worry, the feeling states of our intuitive side are a sense of well-being, hope, joy, and deep compassion. The mind will think it's stupid to feel this way since there is danger out there. Your intuitive side says: *Trust the universe; you will always be cared for in some way.*

Our lives are composed of the moments we live. Unfortunately, many people die on their jobs every day since they are not present to live their own lives. They are thinking about their lives, rather than living them, and their life's essence is deadened as a result. Being intuitively guided, even for a few moments, allows you to awaken to your most authentic self and to realize you're okay. And everything, in time, will be okay, too.

We do still need our mind's intelligence, as well as intuition. Relying on intuition alone, you could be impractical, disorganized, and so unconcerned about what the world thinks that you'd suffer. You might be so connected to the ethereal world that your presence in this one is a struggle. You could be unrealistic and over-trusting, forget where you parked your car, or lose your keys, glasses, or wallet. You might have passion and dreams but never take action since you can't access your mind power. Most people I meet don't need to worry about going overboard on the intuitive side. Instead, they are steeped in the mind. If you feel stuck in your intuition, the next chapter, "Create Structure to Stay Focused," will help you.

Synchronicity and Coincidence

Lisa's coincidence was that her friend's company needed another software representative. I find that when people are working in a direction that's good for them, there is often an uncanny synchronicity.

I had a client, James, who came to coaching feeling depressed, anxious, and unable to see any possibilities. We looked at his behavioral style, talked about his internal barriers, and then worked on his thinking. In this process, he came up with the idea that he wanted to go into animation, to be a cartoonist. Chicago isn't a great market to find a job in this field, but he felt this could be a way of pulling in his creative side. He loved drawing and was pretty good at it. It certainly seemed like an option worth exploring.

James adopted a constructive attitude and said that rather than worrying, he would work on this one day at a time and otherwise live his life. One night he decided to do something fun and different, so he went to a comedy club. While out, he met up with some friends and agreed to follow them to another place. At first, he couldn't get a cab and had to wait. So when one pulled up, he shared it with someone who had also been waiting for a cab. In a five-minute chat before he got to his destination, he found that this woman worked for one of the few animation firms in Chicago. She gave him her card and he followed up during the next week. Chance? Luck? Maybe, but this type of thing happens much more than you'd guess.

Creative Flow

Flow means the ideas come easily; you have rich access to insights and connections. It's an exhilarating feeling. You have only to listen to and honor the ideas that come. For example, the words you need for your résumé are there, and the letter you need to follow-up on an interview almost writes itself.

Ernest Hemingway must have done much of his writing in this creative flow. He's been quoted as saying that when he started to be the one writing the story, he knew it was time to stop for a break. He didn't feel in charge of the writing, a story wrote itself. In writing this book, I've experienced some moments in creative flow. It's a blessing and one of the most satisfying experiences I could have ever imagined. In it, if I listen I can hear what's next and what I need to do. The work unfolds. That's what we all need to do—take steps, go forward, listen to ourselves, be guided, and move effortlessly.

Heart Energy

As I searched to understand the subtle pattern in my clients' success, I came across information that made things suddenly clearer. I attended a workshop presented by a company called Heartmath™. I learned that the electromagnetic energy from the heart area is forty to sixty times stronger than that from the brain. When you activate appreciation, or positive and loving feelings—heart feelings—that heart energy increases and awakens your intuitive intelligence. I believe that when my clients worked on their goals, those who learned how to manage their mind and negative thinking were those who were able to cultivate heart energy. What I was feeling as

I sat across from them was the shift in their energy; they exuded more heart energy from deep positive feelings of appreciation in their lives. This allowed them to access their own intuitive intelligence as well as to influence others positively, whether that involved seeking a new job or managing tough employees. As I picture the situation and how it felt, that makes complete intuitive sense.

Feeling your heart energy isn't hard; it's likely that you already do it, you just don't realize it. For example, you may feel your heart energy increasing when you see a tiny baby, someone you love, a touching movie, or when you hear a story that arouses your sympathy. The best example I have is of ET, the extraterrestrial in the Steven Spielberg movie. ET loved Elliott, the little boy, and was sad about leaving. As he experienced these feelings, his heart glowed in his chest, radiating love.

Bringing heart to your career transition will help you find your intuition and make positive connections with others along the way. I had an interview recently for a television program on the effects of long-term unemployment. To prepare myself, I called the administrator of a large job support organization to see how things were going with their clients. My friend Nancy said: "Our people are definitely taking much longer to find jobs, no doubt there. Instead of a couple of months, it's three months or even longer. Oh, of course, there is always the occasional person who's very positive—things go quick and well, and they breeze out of here in three weeks." I thought, *heart energy.*

CHALLENGES IN CULTIVATING INTUITIVE INTELLIGENCE

So how do you hone this powerful intuitive intelligence? First, a couple of challenges to accessing your intuition—your behavioral style will come into play, and the success you experience one day might very well vanish the next.

Behavioral Style Makes a Difference

Accessing your intuition is likely to be easier for people with certain behavioral styles. I see each of the styles we discussed in chapter four as having their own struggles in the balance between mind and intuition in daily life. For example, the fear-motivated High D (Dominance) and High C (Conscientiousness) behavioral styles might struggle with intuitive connection, but not with drawing upon the mind in planning and goal setting. The friendly, more trusting High I (Influence) and loyal High S (Steadiness) types might naturally gravitate toward the intuitive at the expense of logical considerations.

We each have our own style we live by most naturally. Understanding yours will help you manage your actions in transition. For example, I am a High I (Influence) and if everything is fine, I'm friendly and happy, and it's easy to feel intuitively guided. Under stress, my High D (Dominance) and High C (Conscientiousness) can kick in and I can become perfectionist and rigid, intolerant of ambiguity. *I need to know everything right now!* The little voice of intuition goes on mute. Through trial and error, I've learned that reacting to others from those attitudes doesn't always work that well. In career transition, that's what we can hope for—awareness of our styles and the ability to use that awareness.

Intuition: Here One Day, Gone the Next

Learning to connect with your intuitive and spiritual side is not the same as learning skills like speaking a foreign language or how to drive. You can find the way to intuitive guidance one day, and then the next day it's gone without a trace. It's like one of those movies where the aliens come through a portal but the portal closes up in such a way that you don't know where they came from or how they'll return. We all need practice in keeping the portal open to intuition.

I see this with my clients; some days they are resilient and hopeful, even those who are unemployed for very long periods of time. They are in tune with themselves, creative, confident, doing their part, and not worrying about what they can't control. The next day, they are anxious and depressed. What changed? They did. Their mind went into fear overdrive and is now terrorizing them with worry.

HOW TO STRENGTHEN YOUR INTUITION

Most people get their sharpest insights and discoveries about what they want to do next while doing things like taking a shower or jogging. Could it be that easy? Go for a jog and then know what's next? The reality is that they usually have spent time clearing their channels. They have prepared their minds and hearts to hear what they need. With that clarity, it's possible for the lightning bolts to strike.

The following are attitudes, tools, and exercises I recommend for strengthening your intuition. Pick a few of these and practice them. At first, you may get glimpses of your intuition through an increased positive sense of well-being. With consistent practice, your personal clarity, strength, and insight will improve.

Work, but Don't Struggle

Lisa had been working many, many hours. The cumulative result was that she was too tired to sleep or to make good decisions about how she was actually spending time. She thought since she was always tired that she must be working very hard. In reality, she wasn't working all that effectively but was too tired to realize that.

If you are fortunate enough to have a strong work ethic, it's easy to believe you must work extremely hard to make things happen. But consider that you might be trying too hard to do what you're doing—such as deciding what you want to do with your career, finding your next job, getting your next interview, or discovering your strengths. If that is the case, stop. Do your part, give it absolutely your best energy, and then let it go. Work on something else; there are plenty of tasks to work on in career change. If you persist, you might create your own small world or Chinese handcuff. Trust the universe, God, or whatever you consider your higher power. Strive not just for actions, but *inspired actions*. After you've done your part, give things an opportunity to come to you. You can't "push the river"; certain things bigger than us have their own flow. If you're in the river, you can either flow with the current or paddle upstream.

Breathe

Especially if you feel angry and resentful, mind lock can set in. To increase your ability to unlock the mind and connect with your intuition, breathe in deeply and then exhale s-l-o-w-l-y. Feel your breath fill your abdomen, chest, and then nasal cavities. As you exhale, imagine a moment where you felt deeply appreciated, loved, and cared for. Picture it in detail. Activate these warm feelings in your heart. Feel the strength and warmth deep within your chest. Visualize your heart radiating energy. As you breathe in and out, slowly and deeply, feel this blissful power coming from your chest. Continue this breathing sequence; gently cultivate this feeling for one minute to start with. Work up to five minutes in one sitting. Try this three times a day. Try this in situations where you previously reacted with fear. Breathing can help you change how you feel and act in such situations.

Send Good Energy to Others

Our exchanges with others can help us create or stay in a good zone of intuition. If you're in a tense situation, try the breathing exercise above only once you've cultivated good energy. Then see if you can send this energy to others. Be sincere in your intentions. Think about them in kindly and appreciative ways and direct your harmonious energy to them. You might practice with people you don't know, like in coffee shops or the grocery store. The people I know who do best in employment interviews are those who seem to send good energy naturally. They like others and others like them. They get along. I sometimes use this technique in team-building to break the subtle patterns that can become ingrained in the way people relate to each other. We are all affected by energy in ways we may not quite understand. Being aware of and sending good energy will help you increase your consciousness about this important aspect of life.

Connect with a Power Greater than Yourself

Connecting with intuition is connecting with your spirit. I'm not saying, be religious. Most people have their own name for and conception of what a higher power is. For Lisa, this meant finding and going to a new church. She lost her religious community when she moved to Chicago. In her crisis, she made it a priority to find time for this even though it wouldn't be quite the same as her group from home.

Whether it is your higher self, intuitive self, God, nature, your family, or even groups you belong to, connect with that power. It doesn't have to involve bright lights or burning bushes. Think of who or what your higher power is and spend time cultivating that relationship. Also, think about who or what you are currently worshipping. How do you spend most of your time? What do you give the most reverence and care to? It occurred to one of my clients the other day that his main devotions involved his computer and his personal organizer. He loved fussing over them and spent hours with them. He felt insecure without them. This realization allowed him to make conscious choices that were more in line with what he wanted his life to be.

Pray

For many people, prayer will be the strongest way to make that connection with a higher power. Prayers can be as simple as: *God, help me!* I've met people who found that a morning prayer changed their whole day. It allowed them to let someone or something else be in charge while they did their part. Host Robin Robinson once mentioned on *Good Morning America* that she said a special prayer every morning as an important part of her day. The next day she reported that hundreds of people had contacted her after the show via email and shared their own prayers or asked for a copy of hers. Making a morning prayer your ritual, even if it only takes five minutes, can help keep your intuition flowing.

Visit Nature

Since I have a series of spiritual practices I do daily, including prayers and meditation, I thought I understood spirituality. Then one summer I went on a driving trip along the northern California coast up to Oregon. There are over 84,000 acres of redwood trees that range from 250 to 1000 years old. I can still close my eyes and see the acres and acres of lush beauty, those millions of old, green, silent giants. It's humbling. When you consider the wonders of nature, you realize that we understand so little. Each redwood tree has a root system that is only about five to six feet deep. But intertwined, they create a strong web that allows these beauties to grow more than thirty stories high. Knitted together, they grace the coastal land. Embracing the majesty of nature can certainly make you realize there is a power greater than yourself.

Many people's lives have been changed by doing outdoor growth challenges such as Outward Bound. Clients have said that even taking care of their plants has a calming effect. One young woman I knew who couldn't decide what to do with her future did a trek of the Arctic Circle. A plane dropped her and some fellow travelers and they scaled the wilderness to explore nature and find themselves. Even walking through a public park can shift your focus and reinforce a connection to your intuitive side.

Lastly, consider the elements of fire and water. People throughout time have stared at them for wisdom. Think about it. Have you ever sat by a campfire? Or looked at the ocean? Doing either is calming and mesmerizing; it makes you feel so good. Even talking with someone while sitting on the beach, it can be hard to look away from the ocean. Many of us love being near a fireplace. Perhaps it connects us not only with our own wisdom, but also that of earlier people who stared in the same way.

Pull Inspiration from Your Heroes

One question I often ask people in first sessions is who they admire, who they'd like to be like. If they have heroes—and many people do—when they answer this question, their spine will straighten. They sit up a little taller and prouder. I believe you can be inspired to be more when you think of your heroes. You are reminded of who you want to be and get energy from that vision.

What helps me stay inspired is that I calm myself down. I've been reading Max Lucado. His first story was on Beverly Sills, or "Bubbles." No matter the adversity in her life, she's happy. My focus is to remember that. I can control that.

Chandra, late thirties, attorney, terminated three months ago, just started to search for a new position

We all need someone to inspire us when our own ability to manage a situation is unsteady. It's valuable to ask yourself whom you admire the most and imagine that you have their most admired traits. Give some thought to the people you admire most. Who are they? Make a list and focus on why you admire them.

Try Automatic Writing

In career development workshops, I sometimes have people do automatic writing. I give them a specific time frame—like five minutes—and then hit a stopwatch. I say, "Write down whatever comes to your mind; don't stop writing. I want to see your pencils moving the whole time." Sometimes people write things like: *I am writing for five minutes. I am moving my pen. I don't know what to say.* Even this is good. It brings you to the present moment and in the moment you can find your voice. Working with present voice can bring you an honest and deeper view of yourself. Even if it starts with the realization that automatic writing is a new experience for you and you feel awkward.

While people do believe that writing by hand is the best way to get to your intuition, others love the sound of their fingers on the keyboard. They feel a sense of progress and creativity. I say do it on the computer if you like. I try to do automatic writing for at least 750 words a day. Word count is such a nice feedback tool.

After a couple of pages of automatic writing I can access my intuition much better. It usually takes that much to slog through mind talk—blaming, resentments, and general complaining. I know when I hit the intuitively based insights when I feel calmer, more generous and understanding of others. Ranting and raving on paper can get you safely to your intuitive self.

Some people do recommend writing first thing in the morning. Writing before you go to sleep is also a great idea. It can help you sleep more peacefully, since you get everything off your mind. Also, at night if you are tired your defenses may be down, which can allow you to get a more solid connection with your deepest self and sense of purpose.

Say the Magic Words

Be the "Thank You King." I never thought that much about it until Diane suggested it, but now people call and thank me for the thank you.

Daniel, mid-twenties, account representative for a temporary agency, salary $30,000, looking for job and career change for the last nine months

When we are operating from our intuitive side, we tend to be grateful. And practicing gratitude is one of the most powerful tools we have for accessing our intuition. Stressed and disconnected? Try making a list of ten things you are grateful for. It could begin with small as well as large things. Examples:

- I had a good lunch today.
- I have a warm bed to sleep in tonight.
- My parents are well.
- I am well and not sick.

Listing five things a day you are thankful for can change your attitude and your life. I have seen that people best develop more of what they want when they cultivate deep appreciation for what they currently have.

Play and Have Fun

Your intuitive side is creative and likes to play. In transition, you can easily forget how to have fun. Having fun will help you see yourself and your situation from different angles, which can help you solve problems better. Besides, it could link you to a good career. For example, one of my clients worked months on being more effective at his corporate marketing job. In our work, he became more in touch with his love for playing with his children and, in fact, all children. One day in the shower, it occurred to him to buy a toy store! Last I knew, he owned two stores and loved every minute of his job.

Another example: I worked once with a woman who had taken piano lessons for many years while she was growing up. She was certain piano would not be her career but she loved it. We worked on what to do with her business career and got nowhere. Her mind was stuck. So, I asked her if she could find some time in her schedule to play piano, just for fun. She needed a way to hear her more creative self. She found time to play and started to feel a sense of possibilities again. One summer, she was the pianist for a community musical production. This led her to some contacts and a job she also loved doing—fund-raising for another non-for-profit that needed her creative and outgoing spirit.

Lisa felt like she didn't have any time for fun. However, she came across a friend who got her started back at an old hobby she had in high school—knitting. She joined a group of young professional women who get together and knit once a week. The thought of these thirty-something female lawyers, bankers, and sales professionals all knitting together is heart-warming. She said it calmed her mind and gave her a chance to meet other people. Since she traveled a lot, a knitting project was something she could bring along to relax with.

I would encourage you to do fun things. One guy I know got a model airplane kit and spent more time hitting baseballs. Sports are great for many. The spa route is good, especially for women. However, your fun doesn't have to be expensive—go rent an old comedy and laugh and laugh, or buy a coloring book and crayons. It's good for you and helps you connect with the spirit and deep passion most people long for in their work.

Enjoy Music

Listening to music can be an excellent way to strengthen your intuition. Music can have a direct line to your spirit. The best music might be the kind that helps you want to be better than you are. Or maybe music simply takes your mind off your concerns and therefore lets you hear your little voice better. I love Oprah's concept of the Party of One, where you close the drapes, put on your favorite tunes, and sing and dance all by yourself. You see yourself, you are strong, you are great, and you are *you!*

Years ago, I lived in an apartment where, in the summer with windows open, everyone facing the courtyard could hear each other's music. Every Saturday before noon we were all treated to an "I Am Woman" serenade by a young female tenant in one of the garden units—clearly an empowering song. I looked forward to it.

Try Meditation

Meditation can be an extremely powerful tool. It can help you find a zone to get in tune with yourself and stay inspired, sane, and productive. And it can do even more.

Some of us were raised in environments that hard-wired our brains to have strong emotional and mental reactions to stress. The intensity of early stressors created deep neural patterns. Meditating can help reprogram these reactions and improve your sense of personal coherence, peace, and well-being. It can also help you to become more intuitive. These periods of calming yourself can help uncoil your brain's habitual panic reactions. This has been my personal experience and I have seen it work with others too.

How To? You Already Are

How to meditate? First, start with where you are. Meditation doesn't have to be exotic and ethereal. When I first talk with people about meditation, I ask them what they do that is calming yet absorbing, that gives them pleasure and a sense of timelessness. They typically say things like yoga, writing, cooking, fishing, walking, playing the guitar, or sitting silently outside with their coffee first thing in the morning. Those are forms of meditation since they entail stilling the mind, bringing yourself to the moment, and moving into the calm bliss behind the chattering mind. So, you may do more meditating than you thought! One of my clients says she thinks God is in steam, since every time she takes a sauna, she gets a big download of intuition.

Yet, formal meditation is also a good tool. You can do it in many places and don't need equipment. If you have never meditated in a formal way, it could be good to learn how to meditate from a calm guru or leader. However, you can also learn from someone who never dreamed she'd be doing this, like me. I began about eight years ago after a friend of mine had a stroke. He started a regular meditation practice at a Buddhist Temple near our house. So, I went with him. Here's what I've learned.

Yes You Can! It's Easier than You Think!

Meditation can be easy. The Dalai Lama has said that if a person meditates only five minutes a day, this could make a significant difference over time. So take five minutes; sit in a quiet place where you won't be disturbed. Try to sit in the same place every time and—if you can—use that place only for meditation. Put a clock in front of you. Close your eyes, if you can, and just breathe for five minutes. Your mind might race and start talking to you about everything—*This is stupid, why do this? Is five minutes up? Where are my keys? What will I do today? What did my boss really mean when he said that?* In response, just breathe and focus on your breath—your chest and abdomen filling and emptying. Focus on the magic of air going in and out of your body. Mind still goes, *Am I doing this right? What's the result of this? What time is it?* Just breathe.

I used to think the trick was that I'd get so good at this that my mind would stop talking and I would slip into Nirvana, whatever that was. My newest insight is that no one's mind stops talking. The key is that you don't have to listen. It's like looking into a still forest pool. As you settle down, you can see the fish swimming. The fish don't go away. If you're still and calm, you can see them better. In meditation, you can see your thoughts but you don't have to act upon them. Doing this regularly will help you strengthen your connection to your intuition. You'll realize your mind likes to talk; it has its own patterns and songs. But remember, you are not your mind, you are more than your thoughts. Try it! Certainly you can meditate for longer than five minutes. However, those five minutes can be very powerful.

If you want to learn more about meditation, I have listed my favorite meditation books in the Resources appendix.

Consider a Spiritual Retreat

Several years ago my husband and I decided to plan our summer vacation time the way I help people plan their careers. First, we made a list of what we didn't want. It seemed all too often we went on vacations where we ate too much, spent too much, or filled our time with so many obligations that we didn't have a chance to rejuvenate ourselves. We'd be so stressed out when we came back that we needed time to recuperate.

We agreed that we wanted to do something healthy and spiritual, with the opportunity to spend time outside. We wanted to be able to meet new people, and have good conversations and the chance to learn new things. We decided to take a spiritual retreat and easily found a place on the Internet—a yoga retreat center in Northern California. There is a large collection of sanctuaries—I'm not talking about glitzy health spas, although those sound nice too—that meet many different specifications. There are even ones where you can live for an extended period of time and work in exchange for your accommodations.

I'll never forget the uncommon pleasure of my first silent breakfast, sitting near the fireplace in the dining room. It was such a relief to not have to study a menu at every meal or figure out a tip for everyone who was nice and helped us. I became leaner and stronger in a week without even thinking about food, other than how good it was. Best of all, we had no phone or email for a week and did yoga twice a day. My personal clarity and sense of purpose increased. I never had such a strong sense of well-being in my whole life. I long to return there, and we do for a week almost every year.

In transition, consider a sanctuary time for yourself. Take the pressure off even for a few days if you can. It doesn't have to be expensive. Many retreat organizations have a religious bent but welcome people from all perspectives.

Practice Visualization

Visualization is one of the most powerful tools for cultivating and using the power of your intuition. It is commonly used in sports psychology to enhance peak performance of athletes. Players prepare for difficult situations by first relaxing and then imagining themselves in rich detail executing the actions that will achieve their success. They feel their way into it. Similarly, in martial arts training, you can practice fight sequences by just imagining yourself doing them. Your brain learns the sequences and your muscles know their way back to them much better if you imagine them first.

You can do the same. Create in your own mind your success, your best life and career. Begin by writing out what your ideal work would look like. Who would you be working with? Where would you work? What would you do? What would you wear? Then imagine yourself doing it. How much would you make? Who would be there? What would it feel like? Free your mind and just dream—daydream. Take five minutes and imagine yourself in your ideal work.

If you get stuck and are unable to create images, try again tomorrow. Between now and then, think about ideal work situations. Put yourself in the observer or reporter role. Look at others in their work, on television, in magazines, and as you make your way through the day. Make mental notes. It may take time to create your vision, like putting together pieces of a puzzle. Be patient. Don't let your inner critic get the best of you. Settle for small impressions. If you do this and other exercises from above, the images will definitely come. These images will be better than anything. I believe that creating a vision is essential in managing career change. Often you get what you imagine, so imagine good things for yourself.

Most people use a number of different strategies to connect with their intuition. My best advice is to select two or three activities to do regularly. Also, try to do at least one activity each day, even if you don't feel like it. I find while writing that some days I don't want to do the necessary work to stay in touch with my intuition. I convince myself I'll always feel in flow and don't need to take time away from my work. Pretty soon, everything around me is grating—the noises on the street (why does everyone in Chicago have to honk when they drive?!), the guy sitting near me who just cracked his knuckles, and my slow computer. Also, I start worrying about little things. *What did she mean by that?* Time for beefing up the routine again: visualize the outcome I want, meditate, write, or see a fun and inspiring movie. I saw *Seabiscuit* twice while writing the last two chapters! More on how to stay focused in chapter eight.

WRITING REFLECTION EXERCISES

1. What ideas were most useful to you in this chapter?

2. How would you describe your level of intuitive connection now? How is that working? Are you satisfied with it?

3. Which of these practices to develop your intuition do you currently do?

4. What activities would you like to try to develop your connection?

5. Make a plan for the activities you will be doing to hone your intuition in the next week. Be specific.

CHAPTER EIGHT

CREATE STRUCTURE
TO STAY FOCUSED

Usually, morning is the time to procrastinate. I just do not want to get out of bed—not all that unusual, but it's worse now. Breakfast is fine but trying to go on from there is tough, especially since my house is a mess. The mess outside me makes it difficult to focus. I try making a list and then lose the list. Sometimes I get one thing done and then almost always a second follows. It's that first step that gets me started. When I am feeling overwhelmed and angry I try to resolve these feelings through straightening out the house and getting out the anger.

Fanny, early sixties, solutions engineer who involuntarily left her position three months ago and had been considering a job change for several months, salary $70,000

W hen you're changing careers, you have a lot to do even if you don't have a job. You may be deciding what you want to be for the rest of your life, or at least for your next job; navigating the Internet; making calls to people you do not know; writing thank you notes; trying to network when you'd rather not be talking with anyone; and talking to the answering machine of someone you had called days ago, who returned your call after you stepped out for only five minutes to walk your dog. How do you stay focused, motivated, and productive with these and other challenging tasks? Almost all of my clients say that staying on track and focused is the most difficult task of their transition.

This chapter is designed to help you shape your environment and life so that staying focused will be easy and rewarding and not something you continually struggle with, as many do. The following sections will help you to appreciate the hidden challenges to staying focused, frame your real job while searching for a new one, understand when and why being unfocused can be truly essential, increase awareness of your physical environment and the less than obvious things that may be eroding your concentration, and enhance your energy through the wisdom of an ancient Chinese philosophy, Feng Shui. This chapter will also present a collection of less exotic but still powerful, behavioral and psychological tips from me and my clients. Overall, this chapter will give you a number of action tools to help you cultivate momentum, while increasing your sense of confidence and well-being. It will help you to stop wasting time and get where you want to go.

WHY FOCUSING CAN BE SO HARD

Some of the reasons focusing can be so hard are less obvious than others. To start, career change requires an incredibly high level of self-motivation. Generally, you're the one who decides how you'll work. You determine if you spend more of your time responding to classifieds than contacting recruiters. You also have to develop your own schedule for doing individual tasks, such as completing your résumé.

How long should this take? I'm frequently asked that question. The truth is that the time it should take to do certain career change activities—such as deciding what you really want to and can do, or networking for job leads—is relatively undefined. Without benchmarks, or with misconceptions about the process and timing, you can easily derail yourself. It's hard to determine if we are making real progress. A new client's comment during her first session illustrates this point:

Diane, I have a résumé and I applied to four jobs on Monster.com two weeks ago. I didn't get one response; I'm so depressed! I'll never get a job!

In reality, using only an Internet strategy is an unwise plan. And not getting a response in two weeks is certainly no reason to get depressed and think you'll never get a job.

Further, our jobs can be a little bit like the blinders on a horse—they focus us even if we don't like them. Many of our daily routines, how we see ourselves, what we do that's fun and rewarding, and even our social connections are often structured by our work. Perhaps it isn't fulfilling or positive, but it still takes our time and energy. If you are trying to make a career change while still employed, it may be hard to break out of the consuming patterns of your current job to figure out what to do next. Most people who leave their work, whether voluntarily or through being laid off or fired, need time to create a new balance in their lives. When this structure is gone, we often need some time to get our bearings before we can clearly focus.

Those who are unemployed can feel disoriented without the structure of the work day. In career transition we must create our own structures to maintain our focus.

THE BEST WAY TO APPROACH YOUR CAREER SEARCH

When you commit to looking for a new position—especially if you are unemployed—the search is best considered its own job. This creates an important structure for you. Whether you are working or not, considering your transition as your job, even a part-time one, does have advantages. As with a job, the concept of limiting how much you work on your transition has merit. I find that clients who work fewer than twelve hours a week on their transition have a difficult time maintaining momentum. Conversely, some people overwork. They start with a frenzy of letters, calls, and networking, believing they need to work on it all the time, including evenings and weekends. They forget that everyone needs days off and time for fun and relaxation, and they are allowed to take a break. It's also hard to make good decisions and create positive impressions when you are stressed out. I recommend that you work no more than thirty-two to forty hours a week on your career transition.

Since it's your job, and you set your own schedule, you can also give yourself perks. As one of my clients said recently:

> If I can do this any way I can best manage it, I'll work very hard for four days a week and take off Fridays to sit on my boat. Now *that* sounds like something I'd love to do.

WHY BEING UNFOCUSED SOMETIMES IS IMPORTANT

It's important to understand that periods of time not focused on the process of making a career change can also serve important functions. I'll call this being *unfocused* even though it may involve being focused on something else besides the job search. For at least some people, the transition process also involves a certain unfolding of themselves, which can allow them to reclaim their energy if their last position was stressful. One of my clients who had just spent twelve years in a demanding retail management job that did not fit her talents told me:

> Yes, I took some time away. It was the first two-day weekend I've had in a long time. It feels strange, but I gotta start getting a life. I need a life so I can figure out who I am. Then I can figure out what I should do.

That weekend and other such activities will likely be a valuable part of her career change process.

I wrote earlier about what happens when square pegs leave round holes. These people need time to reclaim their skills and develop new areas of competence. Further, new parts of yourself can also emerge at different points in life; you need to learn more about them to decide if they might be featured in a new career. For example, many people I see at mid-life want different things from a job than they did two decades before. They have a stronger need to do work that is consistent with their values and to be more creative.

These clients can get to know themselves better when they have unfocused time away from their career transition activities.

Unfocusing can take different forms. In some circumstances—for example if you are completely exhausted and have no idea what you want to do with your career—taking a vacation, a break, or a sabbatical might be a beneficial strategy. If it's not feasible, or your anxiety increases just thinking about not having paid work, you may want to consider taking a less demanding, temporary job before making another major work commitment.

Similarly, on a day-to-day basis, we all need the balance of focusing on the tasks we need to get done and then unfocusing to tend to our lives—body, mind, and spirit. In a career change, this is essential. Without it, it's impossible to bring any coherent energy, let alone creativity and resilience, to the work tasks. While some people overwork on their career change, most are likely to say that procrastination is their biggest challenge, and they have spent more than their share of time watching television or mindlessly surfing the Internet.

Balance is sometimes hard to achieve in a career transition; you often have to discover your needs and wants anew, and these may change as you move through the transition. Creating focus as well as balance will help you to discover what makes you tick and feel rested, happy, creative, and productive. The following sections contain concepts and suggestions to help you with that learning process.

FENG SHUI AND FOCUS

My interest in Feng Shui was prompted by some personal and client-related challenges I had confronted. Developed over four thousand years ago, Feng Shui (pronounced *fung shway*) is a Chinese philosophy of placement that continues to help people create environments that support their needs, desires, and well-being. There are various schools that represent different traditions for structuring the environment to enhance the flow of chi, or life force energy. All share the goal of increasing happiness, health, and prosperity.

Feng Shui—which literally means Wind and Water—concerns the structure and content of the living environment: pictures, plants, furniture, the direction different things face, and more. When the Feng Shui of an environment is good, you are likely to feel a sense of calm and peace when you enter it. It can help you feel focused rather than distracted and scattered. In your transition, you can benefit from even simple principles and concepts of Feng Shui without getting steeped in ancient Chinese secrets.

This section about Feng Shui will help you create structure so that you can focus on what needs to be done. First, let me tell you a little about how my experiences with Feng Shui began.

My Dream House Nightmare

In the mid-1990's, my husband and I wanted to sell our house and move to an area of town where we could walk or take a train instead of having to drive everywhere. I teach people how to simplify their lives, and I realized it was time to better practice what I preached. We had already spotted our dream home—a large, vintage apartment in a complex that seldom had units for sale. Coincidentally, one came on the market just when we started to look. The condo had high ceilings and beautiful woodwork; we fell in love with it heart and soul. Fortuitously, we were able to buy it and move in, in short order.

Not long after we moved in, I started to wake up in the middle of the night. I would find myself dreaming while standing up in my bedroom trying to fix something on the wall. My husband slept soundly, except when I woke him up with my talking while I looked anxiously at the wall. The days were fine and we loved the apartment; my bad dreams seemed like a small thing. About the same time, I came across an article about a Feng Shui master who worked with her partner, a Native American Indian healer. I had never looked for help from a Feng Shui consultant before but I decided to give it a try.

When they arrived, yes, they looked a little exotic, but they went right to work. They charted birthdays, where and when my husband and I were born, and documented historical factors of the apartment. They measured and sketched each room and its furniture. They analyzed the energy flow created by the placement of our electrical appliances. They also scanned all the rooms with an electrical device to see if they were haunted by spirits who weren't finished living there. As they sensed and studied the place, a good friend and I answered questions, took notes, and tape-recorded their consultation. Those were our assignments. After three-and-a-half hours, both shared their conclusions and recommendations.

First, no, the place wasn't haunted. My side of the bed, however, was bisected by an energy line created from the right angle of a built-in closet. The corner of the closet faced where I slept, even though I wasn't even near it. At a certain point during the night, my spirit needed to fix it. In Feng Shui, your bed is very important and mine was in a bad place. The masters gave us good marks for colors and energy flow in our new home but made many recommendations that would enhance the chi or energy as we settled in more. Some of these were very easy things to do.

We repositioned our bed to a place that was more auspicious. That, by the way, is a major Feng Shui concept that means good things are more likely to happen. For example, you can have an auspicious address or birth date. One result was that I never had that dream or woke up in the middle of the night like that again. In fact, shortly after moving the bed I was called for an astonishing number of interviews for magazines. For coaches and counselors, getting media interviews is so wonderful. It allows us to share what we do and is the best advertising anyone can get. My colleagues and friends began to tease and quiz me about how I became a media queen. I could only shake my head in wonder and say that I moved my bed.

I've continued to study Feng Shui since, and use its principles combined with common sense when I advise my clients. However, perhaps like you, my strongest insights come from dealing with real challenges. Here's a challenge one of my clients and I had and how using Feng Shui helped.

Clyde's Career Fogginess

I once worked with a very well paid but stressed out quality assurance manager for a computer test-scoring company who wanted to do something different. His job was very routine, structured, and demanding. He wanted a job that was more creative and thought he might want to work in farming or with animals. This was not a simple one-step career solution—it would be a big change. He had a lot of work to do—make contacts, investigate other occupations, and begin to visualize himself doing other things.

One problem to contend with was that Clyde suffered from terrible insomnia. He barely slept at all. It's hard to coach someone to make a big change when he isn't getting enough sleep. It's hard to figure out what is causing what. For example, his job was stressful but it became more stressful since he was tired. He felt foggy about his career, but he was foggy anyway from insomnia.

So, after a few sessions, I began to ask him about where he was sleeping. "Just curious." He began to describe his bedroom. He said he had a normal bed with a big television propped next to it on a barstool.

Coach Diane: TV stand?
Client Clyde: No, a stool—it teeters a little, but I think it's okay. I want to get a better TV stand but haven't. I watch TV if I can't sleep.
Diane: Hmm. . . Tell me more about your room.
Clyde: Under the bed, I have boxes—things from my father.
Diane: Hmm. . . You said you didn't get along much with your father before he died.
Clyde: No, and I really need to read these someday but for now I just keep them under my bed.
Diane: The rest of the room?
Clyde: The biggest piece of furniture is a closet in front of my bed. The doors are usually open since it's filled to the brim. *(Laughs sheepishly.)*

Diane: But Clyde, you seem like a pretty low maintenance dresser. *(I had only seen him in the work shirts and jeans he wore to work every day.)*

Clyde: Well, yes. Those are suits I used to wear when I worked in sales—that job I hated. I don't wear the suits—don't really like them and they don't fit anyway. They make me feel guilty since I was thinner then.

Diane: Hmm . . .

Clyde: My room's pretty cluttered right now since I don't have my taxes done yet and everything's on the desk.

Diane: I think I'm starting to see why you might not be sleeping all that well. Maybe we ought to consider if your room is affecting your sleep and, if so, how to change that.

Clyde: Hmm . . . I was thinking that too.

You don't need to be a Feng Shui master to figure out why he couldn't sleep. Clyde's poor mind and spirit were being nagged all night long, or they were anxiously waiting for his cats to jump on the TV and make it crash on the floor. Clyde made a pact with me that he would clean and clear out his room. He would only keep what was comforting to him. I didn't say to throw out everything, just make a good space to rest. He could organize and store the rest so it would be there when he had more energy to deal with it.

This strategy worked. Soon he felt better, was sleeping better, and became more able to hear his own voice and do the footwork needed to make a change.

USING FENG SHUI PRINCIPLES

The following sections cover ideas on how you can use Feng Shui to help you live and think better and get through the transition process.

Create a Tranquil Sleeping Space

Having a good place to rest is basic for creating good focus in your life. Make boundaries so your resting area is a sacred place; infuse it with tranquility. I advise against locating your career transition materials in your bedroom, especially your computer. If you do have reading materials, put them away before you go to sleep, unless it's a book that's comforting to you. Don't sleep with the television on—that's not good for you. It can fill the layers of your mind with all kinds of information you don't need. Years ago one of my clients went to a sleep clinic for her insomnia. They refused to work with her because she didn't want to turn her TV off while she slept. You do need comfort and clarity in the space around you when you rest—it's the peace factor. If you need sound, try an FM station with soothing music. I suggest clean sheets, nice pictures, and things that make you feel safe, valued, and loved. You may not have an abundance of financial resources in transition, but you can make rich and meaningful choices about what you surround yourself with day and night.

Create Space for Yourself

Another important way to create focus is to make sure you have a space for what you are working on. If you work at home, put the things you need all in one area instead of all over the house. The scattered papers will make you crazy. Some people don't have a desk in their home; they use a table to write on. I encourage you to make a transition briefcase or package that contains everything you need to keep track of what you are doing: phone list, articles on work, or information on companies that you are targeting. You can have it when you need it but put it away when you are not working on it. If you designate an area for the career transition activity, it won't be so hard to get started and keep momentum. You'll train yourself that when you're there, you work on transition. I did that when I was learning to meditate. I made one area of my house the place I meditated. If I sat there, that's what I did. It was easier than finding a place to sit and seeing if I felt like meditating that day.

We are all stimulated—positively or negatively—by what is around us. This includes color, the positive and negative energy of written materials, images, and even where you got the furniture and what it means to you. When you sit in your work area, what do you see? An old picture of someone you dislike? Get rid of it! Look carefully at what surrounds you; everything gives you some type of message. Make sure the messages are encouraging and comforting, not emotionally draining.

Eliminate Clutter

> I have to keep a clean desk and maintain a schedule or to-do list and constantly refer to it. As I finish a task I have to look at the list to see what to do next.
>
> Michael, mid-thirties, consultant, financial services industry, unemployed two months, searching for a new career for one month

I often find that my clients begin a very productive phase of their transition by cleaning a closet, their garage, or the whole house. Odd as it may seem, cleaning seems to accompany or even precipitate change. At times, I recommend cleaning for people who are stuck. They can use organizing as a way of doing "something" on writing projects when nothing else seems to be getting done.

It's amazing that throwing away—or better yet—recycling things you don't want can energize you. Before we moved into our home, we got rid of everything we didn't want or need. It was tremendously liberating. I donated books to the public library, clothes to the Salvation Army, and had a big yard sale. We made a conscious decision about everything we put into our new environment. But if you're like us, the collection of things you don't need or want—things that make you feel guilty or overwhelmed—still mysteriously grows. De-cluttering is an ongoing project for almost everyone.

I have a client whose clutter grew to very significant levels. She couldn't find anything and the mess was driving her husband crazy. To help her get clearer and feel better, she recently committed to de-cluttering her house for twenty minutes a day, five days a week. After one week, she reported she felt immensely better about herself and her life, much more in control. Even de-junking your living space for ten minutes a day could help.

Add Life

Plants, fish, wind chimes, and ceiling fans that circulate air will all enhance the liveliness of your environment. Fresh flowers—or even a single one—for your table or desk add life. Opening the drapes and windows can add to your sense of energy and enlarge your world. It's so easy to feel like a shut-in while in career transition, especially if you are between jobs. Having clean windows to look out of—even if you just clean one window a day—can make a big difference.

Consider Mirrors

Mirrors are the aspirin of Feng Shui. Darkness absorbs chi energy. Since mirrors amplify light, mirrors are used to correct many energy flow problems. Here are some easy things to do. Hang mirrors in dark areas of your home or work area. If you can't see who is coming into a door that's behind you, put a mirror in front of you or on your desk. Our reptilian brains are more likely to relax when we can see who is coming into our space. We all work better when we aren't on edge. If you live up a flight of stairs, having a mirror at the top landing will help draw the energy up to your doorway better. That will give more energy to nourish you in your home. Finally, if you have mirrors that you look at regularly, make sure you can see yourself. Mirrors that chop the top of your head off should be replaced with ones that allow you to see yourself without any effort.

Some Other Feng Shui Tips

Here are a number of actions to consider. First, fix any leaky faucets. Besides wasting a precious resource and possibly fragmenting your concentration, dripping water drains your chi. For this reason, keep all drains closed as well as the lid on your toilet, especially when flushing. In some retreat centers, you'll see signs in the bathroom reminding you to keep the toilet lid closed to conserve chi energy.

Different directions and colors are associated with certain types of energy. For example, when you rest or work, try to position your chair to face east; this is said to increase your ability to see a better future. Since television can numb both mind and spirit, don't sit close when you watch it. Also, putting a live plant next to your TV is thought to increase the energy in the room. North energy is seen as most calming, so make your north-most room your retreat or sleeping room if possible. Yellow is a calming and balancing color. Keeping something yellow in the middle of your living space will help center you; consider yellow flowers or a candle, vase, or pillow.

There is much more to learn about Feng Shui than I have mentioned in the examples above. I've listed additional books in the Resources appendix.

CONTEMPORARY WISDOM TO SHARPEN YOUR FOCUS

While not inspired by ancient secrets, this section will give you other powerful actions to help you get past feeling scattered and disorganized and to sharpen your focus on the job of transition. Many of these suggestions come directly from clients or from a popular coaching program we offered called Reinvent Yourself. Looking beyond your physical environment, these offer ways to create behavioral and psychological structures to increase effectiveness. Keep in mind that the suggestions for conditioning your mind and dealing with your emotions in chapters five and six will enhance your concentration and sense of directedness too.

Change Routines, Make New Rituals

One pet peeve I have is that people want to make significant changes in their careers while keeping all their life patterns the same. This is most likely to occur with people who are employed. They can steadfastly refuse to make even small changes to their schedules and activities and yet want a new life. I have an axiom regarding this: *You can't do everything the same and get different results.* Perhaps this is similar to Einstein's tenet that we can't solve a problem in the same mind in which it was created.

This became poignantly clear to me in coaching one young man who was trying to find a better job. He never found time between sessions to do his homework—take a skill assessment, complete a behavioral style questionnaire, and write his story. Finally, at one session we combed through his entire week's schedule to see where his time went. His week was filled with his favorite TV shows, the night out with the guys, and taking care of his kids at night and on weekends since his wife had them on weekdays.

To make progress, he had a meeting with his family to talk about his career change goal. He enlisted their help on temporary schedule changes. The family members felt they were helping Dad and were also encouraged by the hope that he would be less grumpy if he had a better job. The "guy's night out" part of his schedule is another story.

> The most important thing for me to stay focused is to commit to the development of habits that I associate with change. The most useful tools at this point are meditation, exercise, spiritual reading, journaling, even drinking more water—a commitment to change and improvement.
>
> Aaron, mid-forties, partner in a law firm, undergoing a major career and life transition

The water drinking practice mentioned above came from my company's coaching program, in which we encouraged people to try new things. We suggested they start with some healthy basics such as drinking a minimum of four glasses of water a day. The first day one participant said the only fluid he had before noon was black coffee. He joked that he was changing his body chemistry as he was changing his life. Eventually, it became clear they were related.

Try It! Focusing on increasing your water consumption to eight glasses a day can allow you to reinforce your consciousness of the broader goals. People reported that the cup of water on their desks became a reminder that they were taking small steps to do something different and better for themselves. And through the day, you have a rather tangible way of affecting your system and seeing renewal and cleansing. If you're not a big water drinker, you might just start with a smaller goal, like four glasses. Another Reinvent Yourself participant:

I break up my patterns and go into this creative zone. The journey is good, even drinking water more often makes me feel like I am breaking away from an old routine.

Noel, mid-forties, information technology specialist, current salary $70,000

FEELINGS FOLLOW ACTIONS

It is important to identify and accept your feelings in your career transition, as we discussed in chapter six. However, your emotions are not the only source of your power. In moving through the day-to-day tasks of career change, sometimes you need to just give yourself marching orders to put one foot in front of the other and do what needs to be done. Your actions can change your feelings.

What keeps me focused—if I could ever do that—is to set goals for myself. This is a big challenge; it is difficult to do. Keep busy and don't get caught up in whether you feel like it or not. *Feeling follows action,* not the other way around, which is what I have—action following feeling. I spend too much time figuring out how I feel.

Hal, early forties, scientist, voluntarily left his organization nine months ago

It's very easy to focus too much on your feeling world if you never had much time to do it before your career change. Now you may have more time and are motivated to understand deeply what is important to do before you make the next career move. However, some days need to be Nike Days: "Just do it!"

The following sections contain suggestions for directing yourself into positive activities by engaging your logical mind and keeping it out of fear mode. If you feel stuck and overwhelmed during the day, standing back and then updating your plans can be soothing as well as constructive.

Make Your List on Sunday

The lack of structure in a career transition, especially without a job, can feel most threatening right after the weekend. Strategies for dealing with Monday morning are always a good idea.

Staying focused day-to-day is very difficult because other activities always seem to get in the way. So far, the most helpful thing has been to make a list on Sunday of about three tasks to be done in the next week without too much difficulty.

Brita, early fifties, employed project manager for a small manufacturing firm, salary $40,000, has been searching six months for a new career position

Manage the Mornings

After Monday, there are the other mornings, which can be just as daunting.

One of the hardest times for me is first thing in the morning when I get up and have nowhere to go. To help stay focused I go to the gym—this helps me get up and out. Another thing that helps me stay focused is putting a structure on my day. Even if it's going to meet someone for lunch—it gets me around, and then when I come home I am ready to focus again.

Nancy, late thirties, former director of marketing, terminated two months ago, salary $85,000, actively searching for a new job for a month

Set Bite-Sized Goals

Setting goals is one of the most important tasks in your career transition. If your only goal is to find a new job, you could spend a lot of time feeling unmotivated and depressed. The transition process will take many steps. People who recognize this and break their goals into small steps tend to stay focused and manage transitional stress better.

Set a schedule, do time management, set goals, do one thing each day. Break into smaller bite-sized pieces—one task at a time. Make a list and check off items when completed. Have a purpose in life. Keep learning and be willing to learn.

Gisele, fifty, freelance consultant attempting to significantly redirect and expand her scope of services while coping with the death of her younger brother

I stay focused by realizing everything involves time. Change and transition are going to come about at a certain pace. If I have priorities and major things I want to accomplish, one thing I do is write them down and then work backwards. What steps do I need to do to get there and what order do I need to put them in? Like a set of stairs—several steps to climb.

Rosalie, early forties, assistant editor for a small newspaper, looking for a new position

Create Action Plans

It is important to construct not just goals but also related actions—that's what you will do to accomplish them. Creating these plans is often very soothing since it's easy to get into magical thinking in transition, as though everything is already predetermined in some negative way.

Recently I have spent time developing specific goals and writing them down. I then try to develop action plans to go with each goal. For example, I know that I have a potential interest in writing and would like to explore opportunities in freelance writing. As a starting point, I have enrolled in a writing course at the U of C.

Shanta, mid-thirties, currently a human resources manager for a financial firm, salary $85,000

Create Accountability

Without a boss for the career transition, you need to be thoughtful about how you hold yourself accountable.

> I stay focused by forcing myself to list objectives the day before and to summarize events and accomplishments at the end of each day. This has forced me to physically carry over uncompleted items each day. With this, I become painfully aware of what I didn't attempt to do early enough during the day. Canceling my newspaper subscriptions has also added to my available time.
>
> Paul, former director at a software company, salary $98,000

Some folks create accountability groups with friends and others in transition. They meet once a week and talk about their goals and outcomes. This is an excellent idea. Also, I encourage and sometimes require my clients to email me their weekly "to do" lists. It helps them to formulate their intentions into words and make real commitments. It also helps me to keep a good sense of where they are at. I'm not sure I can completely explain why but I think it is often very important for another person to have the details on "where you are at" in the career transition process. As a coach, I like holding this in my mind for my people.

Celebrate Success

Celebrating your accomplishments—even small ones—is very important for bringing focus.

> Stay focused? An almost impossible task! Celebrate small successes with friends, or anyone for that matter. Celebrate any movement toward your goals, even simple goals like getting up before 8:30 a.m., or eating three meals a day instead of three before lunch!
>
> Madelyn, forty-eight, advertising brand development professional, unemployed for three months

You must bring recognition and joy to what you accomplish along the way! Waiting until you get a job to celebrate is so self-defeating and doesn't reflect an awareness of the many important little and big steps required. You can celebrate by giving yourself a treat like calling an old friend, watching a favorite television show, or doing all your work earlier in the week and taking Fridays off. And yes, many people do spend a great deal of time looking for their next job in the refrigerator. If that describes you, you're not alone. Eating, of course, is a way of managing stress and chapter five can help you with that important topic too. Using some of the structuring ideas in this chapter can also help you with that.

KEEP IN MIND WHY YOU ARE DOING THIS

We talked a lot in about finding a sense of what is best for you in chapter seven. Day-to-day, this is important too. Digging down deep and reminding yourself of the reasons you are making the change, why you have to make progress, and the positive results you intend to create, can significantly align your focus. It doesn't matter what the reasons are. It matters that you know what's important and what your key purpose is. The following sections contain quotes by people who have kept their purpose in mind.

No Regrets

> The force that keeps me focused is that I will regret if I never try. Although I thought about quitting, the fear of regretting keeps me moving on. I prefer to use one year trying rather than have regrets for the rest of my life.
>
> Wung, late twenties, formerly a graduate research assistant, searching for a position in marketing research for the last three months

Family Goals

> Another big thing keeping me focused is my plan to adopt a baby. Knowing that's ahead gives me incentive on several

levels, like needing a steady job with good salary and maternity benefits, but also just knowing that helps.

Erin, early forties, currently a public relations executive for a major municipal public organization, salary $50,000

External Commitments

My advisors need to feel they haven't wasted their time with me. The "excuses" for not having a job get less plausible with each passing month.

Ram, late thirties, former computer engineer who has been searching for a new position for six months

Internal Commitments

I need to concentrate on keeping the following commitments in front of my actions, so that I step into them to live my life:
- my mission
- my heart's desire
- my promises

It's so hard to *be* what I say I want to be and do.

Gwyneth, professor and director for a major university, fifty-six, salary $55,000

Stay Above the Terror

Most people seem to like the carrot approach—working toward some reward like a nice job, financial benefits, or the fulfillment of a lifelong vision. Others, like Joe below, believe they need the stick approach—staying motivated by continually reminding themselves of their flaws and worst fears.

Success breeds success, and some gain seems to keep me moving toward more gain. I do also want to avoid pain, so I sometimes stay on track just to stay above the terror that I imagine will happen if I stall or fail. Wish I didn't have to beat myself up to stay on track. Is there a better way? But it is working for me.

Joe, early forties, voluntarily left position two years ago, completed additional training and is now two months into a search for a new position

Shift Your Work Environment

During your day, one simple idea to stimulate your progress is to change environments to stimulate your work progress. Or you may just plan on working outside your home, if you are not working in an office.

To jump-start my focus sometimes it helps to get out of the house—go to the library—away from the distractions of home.

Hanna, early fifties, terminated from a director-level position in health care six months ago, salary $80,000, actively seeking a new career for the past three months

The library is an excellent place to work on the things that require quiet concentration, like letter-writing and research. Some people do their best reading and reflection in coffee shops. Getting out and changing locations can help break up the day without your having to completely take your focus off working on your career transition.

Stay Connected in Relationships

For many people, like Paul and Gretchen below, relationships will be a motivational key. You see this in the rise of informal job support groups for people in transition. This can be a wonderful thing. Staying in connection with others helps to normalize your life and keep your energy higher.

The biggest thing that has helped me stay focused is having some quasi-career coaches (friends and relatives) who continue to check in with me to see how things are going.

Paul, former director at a software company, salary $98,000

Connecting with people is powerful for me. I am energized and focused by the very presence of others. It's as if things begin to align themselves.

Gretchen, forty-two, regional account manager in advertising, currently trying to navigate a job and career change, salary high $40s

However, it's not always easy to figure out how to benefit from, or even keep, your close relationships during the stress of transition. The next chapter, "Help People Help You," will give you many ideas on that.

CULTIVATE THE POSITIVE

At no other time in your life will your attitude be so important. Positive energy builds a positive focus. The following are simple recipes from my clients for keeping a positive attitude.

Keep Your Contacts Positive

Stay away from negative people.

Teresa, mid-thirties, laid off one month earlier, former senior manager for a communications consulting firm, salary $80,000

Make Yourself Reminders

I have put up positive notes, comments, and quotes in my apartment to give me the encouragement to push onward and succeed. I'm impatiently waiting!

Madelyn, thirty-two, formerly a customer service representative at a payroll firm, attempting to return to work after being fired months ago

Keeping Your Drive Positive

> I have tapes I listen to in my car—inspirational and religious speakers. It helps!
>
> Tammy, early thirties, trying to change careers from image consultant to manufacturer's representative

CREATE EMOTIONAL BALANCE

Many people have their own favorite ways to center and reconnect with themselves. Transition is the time to remember and use these tools and to even expand your tool chest. Doing so will help you sharpen your focus when you need to shift gears and work on the transition tasks, like résumé writing and networking. The suggestions in chapters six and seven on emotions and intuition will be valuable. For inspiration, here are examples of how others stay in balance.

> My best tools are my coach and friends to talk to, to test ideas, to get feedback-strokes and challenge. Other tools include books—both novels and nonfiction—and meditation. Yoga, weights, chocolate, good sex, a creativity seminar, working in paints all contribute to a sense of centering and creating, noticing and speaking. Sunshine helps. So does shopping, candles, incense and nice jewelry.
>
> Gwyneth, mid-forties, instructor and director for an educational institution, salary $55,000

> To center myself at work I call my wife and talk with her. At home, I take the twins out for a trip to the park. But most often I pray to myself—it helps a lot. I try to find time to center myself every day and stay clear of caffeine. Switching from coffee to tea has been a great help.
>
> Ivan, late forties, commodities trader, beginning the process of a job or career transition

Humor is the best! Nothing beats laughing with my friends about the rest of the world. Nothing mean, just finding the humor in life.

Teresa, mid-thirties, laid off one month earlier, former senior manager for a communications consulting firm, salary $80,000

How do you best stay focused on the key tasks? It's not a simple question. Finding your own answer is part of an important learning process—one that will enrich your understanding of yourself and what you need to be happy, as well as give you skills to manage other uncertain passages later on in life. One big factor in our surroundings is our relationships, especially with people who are closest to us, like friends and family. In transition, these relationships can be a mixed blessing. Certainly it's an area of life that is important and must be reckoned with. The next chapter, "Help People Help You," will give you insights and tools to make the most of your inner circle as you work on your job of career transition.

WRITING REFLECTION EXERCISES

1. How would you rate your level of focus in your career transition, right now? Rate yourself on a 1 – 10 scale where 10 means you are extremely focused on the tasks you need to be doing and 1 means you lack concentrated focus. Describe your current level of focus in words. Rating:_____

2. What are you currently doing that is especially helpful in keeping you on track with the work of your career change?

3. What did you connect with in the quotes throughout this chapter? Can you identify with any of them? How so?

4. How do your environment and work space support your transition? How do they detract?

5. What can you do to minimize or eliminate detractors from your process?

6. List three things you can take away from this chapter that will help you focus better.

CHAPTER NINE

HELP PEOPLE HELP YOU

My mother called me three times yesterday asking me when I was getting a job. I told her it's not that simple. I'm trying to figure out what's best for me and make it a meaningful move. The third call was the best. She had found me a job. The neighborhood dry cleaner needs someone and she had talked to the manager on my behalf. This is making me crazy—today I'm not answering my phone.

Janice, forty-four, left her position as an operations manager at a small manufacturing firm a week ago since her position had been eliminated, salary $50,000

When you're in the midst of career change, often the people in your inner circle of family and friends want to help but don't know what to do. Some who have gone through their own career transitions will remember what it was like and what was helpful. Others may not. Even so, remembering their transitions doesn't ensure they'll give you the help you need. And face it, real help could take a number of different forms, including checking in to see how you are, finding job leads, picking up your dry cleaning, or listening to you talk endlessly about what your experience is like.

All of us need help to get through career change. If you are stuck on the idea that you want to be independent and not impose on others, ask yourself these questions: "Would I help others in a career transition?" And, "Could I help them in ways they couldn't help themselves?" Your answers are likely to be: "Yes, of course!" I rest my case.

FOUR STEPS TO GETTING THE HELP YOU NEED

So how do you get help from friends and family in ways that don't drive you crazy? And what if you don't have anyone to jump in and help, even if they aren't all that helpful? These are the questions chapter nine will address. A basic premise of our discussion is that you must take responsibility for your own needs and desires. This is not the time to sit and wish things were different, or to console yourself by saying that if someone really cared they would just do something. We have all tried this and know it doesn't work. Career transition is often hard on your relationships. And yet, this can also be a time for deepening and even expanding your circle of important connections. These four steps will help you:

- Get clear on what's helpful to you.
- Assess the capabilities of your current support network.
- Convey and negotiate your needs.
- Manage your support network.

While there are countless books on business networking, few, if any, dare to deal with the sticky topic of how to get useful support from non-business relationships—our inner circle. Yet these relationships can make the biggest difference in how you progress. In the end, this chapter may be one of the most valuable ones for getting back into control and staying sane, productive, and inspired in your career transition.

Step One: Get Clear on What Helps You

It's easy to think about getting help as an all-or-nothing proposition. You either have all you need, thank you, or you're miserably alone in the career transition. And *our* version of what others could do for us is what *they* should know without even being told. *Help is my idea, and my idea only, of what help should be.* My female clients often say their boyfriends or husbands try to *fix* things for them and give them advice, which they can consider unhelpful or even annoying. These significant others can similarly be frustrated that their help isn't appreciated. *Why can't she see I'm trying to help her?* Since one person feels like they aren't getting help and the other feels like their help is not appreciated, there may be tension and a disconnect. Using global concepts to think about what you need and get from others is often quite limiting. You need to develop an understanding and language to convey more precisely what's helpful to you to stay sane, keep your relationships, and be effectively interdependent with others. And be clear, career change was never meant to be done alone.

To develop a picture of what you need and a language for getting it, step one has two parts. First you will have a rare opportunity to read candid and sometimes intimate accounts of what others have found most helpful and most unhelpful. These could be "do's" and "don't's" for their friends and family. Listen carefully to the voices in the following sections and let them sharpen your awareness. Make notes for yourself on whether or not these apply to you. You also may want to share what you learn from this section with members of your current network to educate them on the do's and don'ts.

The second part of this step is to summarize your insights by making a list of what help you want, what you currently receive, and what you'd like more of. Your task here is to accept and honor what you need. Everyone has his or her own unique needs in career transition. Yours will depend on your stage in the transition as well as your personal history and behavioral style.

The Do's

The following insights answer the question, "What's the most helpful thing anyone could do for you in transition?" What's astounding to me is how different the responses to this question can be. Let's start with the most popular one.

Be a Sounding Board

Time and time again, what people want most in navigating career transition is for their friends and family to just listen. This is especially true for those in the Neutral Zone, where we are like ships moving through uncharted water. Having someone listen to us can make it easier to hear ourselves and navigate better. For many, this will be the place to start. When you're stuck and riddled with emotional insecurities, talk it through with your favorite listener.

I can't believe my friends still listen to me—listen to me analyze, listen to me speculate. Listen to my fears, my frustrations. Listen to my plodding and pathways taken. I can't believe they call back. Comments, sympathy, advice. Their time in this busy world is allocated to a friend with her head buried in a storm. How fortunate I am that they are in my life.

Yael, early thirties, currently employed as a sales manager in the hospitality industry, describing the search for her first professional job

My friends serve as a sounding board when I consider alternatives regarding my career path, suggest resources which I may not have thought of (people to talk to, books to read), or suggest activities we might do to allow me to focus on other things for a change of pace. I get consumed with finding a new job. Maybe most important is for the person to listen when I feel the need to vent, just either out of frustration or because I've come upon a new idea.

Shanta, mid-thirties, currently a human resources manager for a financial firm, salary $85,000

Listening fills a fundamental need in transition and can also provide the basis for these other types of support.

Give Me Permission

We are often waiting for permission from others. We want permission to be who we are, do the next right thing, or choose an entirely new career. It can be a shocking insight to realize this, but worth knowing. And it is true that our friends and family can expand as well as limit the options we seriously consider. At best, they help us open new doors to possibilities we can create.

The most helpful thing someone could do for me in this transition is listen. Listen to where I've been and where I want to go. Then say, "Yes, you can do it"—not in the way of encouragement, but in the way of permission to do that which I've always wanted to do.

Katrine, forty-three, college instructor who has been working on a career change off and on for four years, salary mid $30s

However, I don't recommend that you approach your path into a new job or career looking for permission. Hopefully this permission will come from within in your journey to understand your own special talents, passions, and desires. After doing a good assessment of their career assets, many see a growth in confidence and awareness. Also, doing exercises in chapter seven to tune up the volume on that little voice can get you past the longing to find permission outside of yourself.

Create a New Language with Me

The way that you talk about your transition will directly affect what you do in it, how you feel about it, and inevitably, the results you will get from your efforts. Perhaps in moving away from the language of your previous job world, you will need to define a language to discuss what you offer the market place. In outplacement counseling, I always think a primary function I serve is to help people find the words to describe what they were doing, what they are good at, and what they'd like next. That's not easy to do alone.

My close friend Bill has taken the time to listen to me talk about my transition on a daily basis—it allowed me to purge myself and to sound out a new language, ideas and outlook on things.

Aaron, mid-forties, partner in a law firm, undergoing a major career and life transition

Help Me Clarify What I'm Thinking

Some people are better than others at helping you tease apart your thoughts. More than a shoulder to cry on, they ask questions to help you understand what you mean and to clarify your thinking.

My counselor at the agency asked me a series of questions to help me focus on where the job search could go—she asked what I liked most and least about my assignments. She offered me other help in focusing on what I can say about myself in a concise way.

Maggie, mid-fifties, laid off one month ago from her position of six years as a communications specialist, seeking a career change

My coach's questions have helped me get a bigger picture and to see my starts and stops in a different way. She questions me closely when my thinking is muddled. Her commitment to me and to help me stay focused has been of the greatest importance. It started me on different ways of thinking and has allowed me to think with a clear head.

Daniel, mid-twenties, account representative for a temporary agency, salary $30,000, looking for job and career change for the last nine months

Challenge Me—The Kick in the Pants

Most of us have people in our lives who do more than listen and reflect. They have a tendency to make us face ourselves and take responsibility. We may not always like what they say, but we need to hear them.

My friend Kelly really listens to my ideas about career change. She is supportive of my change but challenges my statements and assumptions. As a result, she keeps me practical and realistic about career planning. If Kelly believes I'm taking the easy way out and settling for something less, she doesn't hesitate to call me on it.

Brita, early fifties, employed project manager for a small manufacturing firm, salary $40s, has been searching six months for a new career position

In a career change, it is so easy to delude ourselves about our progress, what we could best do next, and how hard we are working on the change itself. Challenge doesn't have to be aggressive or mean to be useful.

Provide Feedback—Be a Mirror

Cultivating relationships that allow personal feedback is a valuable thing for many. A key part of the whole sequence of finding a new career position is to understand who you are and what is working. Many clients get lost in their preoccupation with what will happen in their career change and what to do next. This is where we need people from the outside to be a mirror, so we can see what we are too close to see ourselves.

> I am totally amazed when I am talking in circles about not knowing where I want to go and someone will say, "Eva, you'd really be good at . . ." I am surprised that often someone I will be talking to casually can be so clear about what I really want to take seriously.
>
> Eva, mid-forties, health and beauty care professional presently employed but wanting for the past two years to make a change into a career more meaningful to her

Be a Cheerleader

To some degree, everyone in transition needs others who can give them assurance and confirmation. This is especially important in the Neutral Zone when you can feel so alienated and lost. We need to be reminded that there can be a good result from the often strange odyssey of career change activities—an odyssey that involves finding where you fit and what makes you happy.

> I need someone to assure me that the journey, the path of self-discovery that I've chosen, will ultimately bring me to where I belong—not just to where I can continue to be productive and earn a decent or substantial salary, but where I

belong. And the person should add, "It may prove somewhat difficult to be on this journey, but it will be worthwhile."

Richard, early forties, skilled manufacturing technician and part-time college student beginning to search for new position

Encouragement has been freely given and I need that most. Former colleagues and even current co-workers express interest in what I am doing—it spurs me on. When people know you're in the process of reinventing yourself, they take notice.

Encouragement is a boost to self-confidence. My daughter and I discuss situations and she was right on during my assessment interviews with her. She understands a lot without much talk.

Amanda, late fifties, customer services manager, salary $55,000, considering a career change

By "assessment interviews" Amanda is referring to one of the coaching exercises we did. I ask clients to conduct interviews with their friends, family, colleagues and others who know them to collect outside opinions on their strengths, limitations, and ideal jobs. Opening this dialogue with others is often encouraging and provides excellent feedback. Further, it gives key people in their networks a meaningful role in helping my clients.

I guess I need confirmation that I possess these talents, not just that I have them because they appear on the résumé.

Gretchen, forty-two, regional account manager in advertising, currently trying to navigate a job or career change, salary high $40s

Provide Soul Nurturing

In the most intimate circle of our helping relationships are those who help us stay sane and grounded by their presence and deep connection. Transitions are often very isolating. Intimate communication with key others—even if they don't have practical advice or input—is essential for many of us. Relationships that provide soul-nurturing have a spiritual quality to them. These are people with whom we have connections that go beyond time and space, convenience, and immediate geographic situations.

> What I like about Lauren is that she just makes me feel so good. I know she cares about me so much even though she knows how crazy I can feel. I've known her a long time, through thick and thin. I can tell her anything. She'll always be in my life.
>
> Marie, forty-eight, advertising executive, salary $125,000

Give Unconditional Love

During times of transition, having someone lavish you with love that requires no deep thinking and nothing in return can be lifesaving. This love doesn't depend on where you work or live or how much money you make. It is given in your darkest moments of self-doubt as well as your most confident, bright, and shining days.

One client told me recently she loved to spend time with small children—especially her nieces and nephews—after she was fired. She enjoyed their exuberant love as well as their innocence, energy, and unvarnished joy. During these times, many people deepen their attachment to their pets, as they are great sources of companionship and unquestioning love. These connections can allow us to see a bigger picture of life and know that our strongest value is not in what we do or have done, but in who we are. And who we are is perfectly okay.

Be Authentic and Share Personal Stories

For some reason, these actions seem to go together. People who are real about what is happening are also likely to be able to inspire us with their own true stories.

> The most helpful thing anyone has done so far is just to be honest—don't ignore the elephant sitting in the living room, give me honest feedback. Give me real support, ask about how I'm doing, don't pretend it isn't happening. It's horrible

to be ignored! Then tell me your war stories about how you were able to survive such difficult things. It's so amazing and sounds so strange, but I can still remember years later people telling me about the jams they got into and how they had worked at getting out of tough spots and that it came out okay. It was like a movie I was in and I needed to see if it could possibly have a good ending. I thank them.

Gretchen, forty-two, regional account manager in advertising

I pretended I was normal when I felt so lost. It was helpful when people didn't act too strange about how my life seemed to be evolving and said they know other people who had had bad things happen to them too.

Mary, age forty-eight, reflecting on an earlier career loss

Give Me Time and Space

So many times when clients tell me what they want from their family and friends, it's space and freedom from expectations. *Just leave me alone for a while and don't ask me about this.* To be open to learn from your transition journey and to come out stronger, you need a sense of personal freedom. It's hard to be creative while worrying about reporting exactly what you will do and when. Here are some examples of family and friends who gave space.

The Non-Pressuring Wife

My wife took off any pressure of a deadline, and made it clear that finding the right work is more important than finding work right away. This reminds me that often the right things do just take time to develop. It might happen overnight, but it might need time to grow and develop. I'd hate to be impatient myself and in doing so take away a better opportunity.

Joe, mid-forties, voluntarily left position two years ago, completed additional training and is now two months into a search for a new position

The Open-Minded Girlfriend

My girlfriend has not put the least amount of pressure on me around the job search. She has been excited to hear the things I am learning and has even started to journal on her own. She is extremely open-minded. She knows I want change and believes that I will find my way to it. I wish I could show as much confidence in her. She gives me the freedom to choose.

Noel, mid-forties, information technology specialist, salary $70,000

The Husband Who Returns Favors

Most helpful was my husband not hassling me about finding a job. He asks how I'm doing and I can see he is worried at times, but he doesn't talk about it unless I ask him to talk. I feel like he's there, but is biting his tongue. He's said I didn't hassle him when he got fired several years ago and he's returning the favor. I can't expect his attitude to last forever and I don't want to lose his goodwill, so I'm trying not to take advantage.

Hanna, early fifties, terminated from director-level health care position six months ago, salary $80,000's, actively seeking a new career for past three months

Of course, when you've been in the Neutral Zone longer than anyone should be, you may also want these people to become your challengers and give you a kick in the pants to get moving.

Give Me Guidance and Direction

Sage wisdom or even just ideas about what we should do next is especially helpful in the Neutral Zone. We usually have a hard time seeing a bigger picture and this can help us focus better.

One of the most helpful things has been the advice of a friend in our building. She suggested I go into corporate communications and recommended I talk to several of her friends. These were my first informational networking interviews, and

I found these people glad to talk. It was a field I knew nothing about. I will probably not go in that direction, but it was food for thought, and it built my confidence about talking to strangers on the phone.

Nigel, late forties, three months after his leadership position for a large not-for-profit organization was eliminated

Be a Bud

When you leave a job, you leave your co-workers and colleagues. Many find it helpful to have someone to buddy up with from time to time, to be their company on the path.

A very close friend is also going through the same thing. It helps knowing someone else is going through the same thing you are going through. I often will go to her apartment and use her computer since I don't have one yet. It helps both of us to be working on our own stuff in one place. We were roommates in graduate school and working like this brings back old times. Another helpful thing is all the calls people make, just to touch base and see how I am doing. Some days are filled just responding to these personal calls.

Nancy, late thirties, formerly director of marketing, terminated from her position two months ago, searching actively for a new job for one month

Give Me Practical Help with My Job Search

If you think of support as just emotional, you might keep yourself from getting some other help you also need. In fact, some people will be more likely to provide practical assistance than any other type. For example, I was working with a male client whose wife was also in a career transition. He said he'd rather go buy stamps, do Internet research, or even retype her résumé two hundred times than listen to another minute of her disappointment with her last job interview. The next sections are examples of practical support directly related to the job search process.

Practice Interviewing. Interviewing is the toughest thing for almost everyone in a job search. Practicing with another person before the real thing can make a huge difference.

> The most helpful thing was talking to my dad about questions to ask the employer and how to respond to tough interview questions.
>
> Wallace, early thirties, formerly a warehouse manager, voluntarily left his company over two months ago and has been looking for a new position or career

Help Me Construct My Résumé. The résumé is usually a big stumbling block for many. It's easy to get outdated with the technology you'll need to use to create your résumé if you don't work in companies that require continual updating of those skills.

> My younger friend Zoe helped me to put together my résumé. We put it on disk so I can change it as needed. Not having a résumé was a real stopping point for me, and doing my résumé was really the first step I took in beginning my transition.
>
> Jan, early forties, employed floral assistant looking to make a career change, salary $14,000

Suggest Good Books. When there are so many career books and other resources, it can be valuable to have someone narrow down the possibilities for you and inspire you to read a good one.

> My brother recommended a book called *Get Wired, Get Hired.* It covered how to use the Internet in a job search. This led me to the *Riley Guide,* which I have been able to use in my normal search. It has provided nearly an unlimited number of resources. My biggest task is evaluating, remembering, and using all the books I have.
>
> Carlo, late forties, salary $65,000, currently a staff assistant, has been looking for a new position for ten months

Give Me Job or Industry Contacts. Names of people to contact who can directly help the search process are an invaluable resource.

> The most helpful thing anyone has done for me was when my neighbor prepared a list of people who had recently left her consulting firm and had moved on to other positions at competing firms. She wanted me to talk to them about their perceptions of the new firms and the opportunities they looked at in their transitions. She also went into detail with me about how she related to each of these people, all of whom were friends of hers.
>
> Paul, former director at a software company, salary $98,000

Refer Me to Job Networks. Job support groups are often highly valuable, and yet many people do not know about them or need some serious coaxing to attend one. Once you go, you may see what a great resource they are for motivation and contacts.

> My dad told me about job support groups and actually went with me to my first meeting at the Career Transitions Center. It helps so much to know that he is in my corner.
>
> Wallace, early thirties, formerly a warehouse manager

Give Me Practical Help with My Life

In a career transition, most people can use a helping hand that is not directly related to the job search. Your emotional well-being is affected by the practical aspects of life, especially if you have lost your job or left it to make a better life for yourself. Some of us—like parents or single parents—may need more help than others. For example, Janice, whom we met at the beginning of the chapter, is a single parent with two little boys under ten years old. She needed lots of help, but it wasn't to find job leads like her mother was doing. So Janice had a good talk with her Mom, explained the career transition process, and gave her some other ways to help—running errands, bringing the kids to school when she had an interview, and providing a small loan until her unemployment started up. Janice's mother took pride in being able to help her daughter in ways that others could not. This also took away some of Janice's anxiety about what her Mom would do next.

The Don'ts

Thinking that maybe there would also be differences in what people in transition find unhelpful, I asked clients and friends this question, "What's the most unhelpful thing anyone could do for you in your transition?" The answers were resoundingly similar and corresponded with my own experiences with clients. However, these still may help you clarify what is best for you and if you agree, make you realize you're not alone!

Don't Ask the Dreaded Question

Just don't ask me, "So, have you found a new job yet?"

Shanta, mid-thirties, currently a human resources manager for a financial firm, salary $85,000

This is the universal "don't"! It's such an illogical question too, when you consider that if the job seeker had found a new job, he or she would most likely tell you without you asking. Many people in transition will find this shame-inducing. They will hear it as, "What's wrong with you?" If you do want to help a job seeker, it is better to say, "How can I help you?"

The most helpful people have been those who have refrained from asking me if I have a job yet and who have validated my desire not to do anything for a while—people who have been open to having fun with me.

Hanna, early fifties, terminated from director-level health care position six months ago

Don't Nag

"What have you been doing all day?" "When will you get a job?" "Haven't you been working on this long enough?" No one needs or likes nagging, nor will it make the situation better. People in transition, especially those without a job, can feel they have very little control over their lives. To undercut their sense of progress or try to control their job search process can add stress. If you want to help someone, you could offer to be a sounding board or to give guidance and direction. Ask for permission before helping, and specify the kind of help you'd like to give before you launch into it. That will help the person in transition feel more in control and be open to your input.

Don't Be Critical or Judgmental

> My brother told everyone I was not focused on the job search—what the hell does he know?! My siblings tend to be so judgmental.
>
> Fanny, early sixties, solutions engineer who involuntarily left her position three months ago and had been considering a job change for several months, salary $70,000

Regardless of your past successes, it's easy to feel "not good enough" or like you'll never get past where you feel stuck. If the people around us are judgmental, it can feel even worse. Often our worst critics are those whose own worst fears are about their sense of inadequacy or inability to make changes. If you feel criticized and it starts affecting your self-esteem, be sure to do the exercises in the section of chapter five called "Ideas for Strengthening Your Identity and Self-Esteem." Don't let it get the best of you.

To complete your work on step one, summarize your insights from the quotes and comments above. Be aware, each person will have their own unique pattern of needs. For example, I have met people who only wanted practical career change help from their inner circle, such as input on their resume or interviewing skills;

others who just wanted a pal they could have fun with; and still others who could solve any practical or person problem on their own after they found someone who would listen to their concerns. Make a list of what help you want, what help you already get that you need, and what you'd like more of.

Step Two: Assess Your Support Network

Examine the strengths and limitations of your current support network. First, list all the members of your network: friends, colleagues, family, and acquaintances. For some people, the list may be surprisingly long or short. Day-to-day, especially when working full time, we all tend to keep ourselves very busy and our world can get small. Unless we're in crisis, we seldom think about our emotional and practical support network.

You need to ask for the right kind of help from the right people. Be discerning about who you are asking to do what. Just as Janice's mother felt she could do anything for her daughter, it can be easy to think your significant others should be able to help with anything that comes up, whether it's advice on interviewing, or on your résumé, or help deciding what you want to do. That is likely to result in a misuse of your time and theirs if they are not experts in the career transitions area. Even if they are, they are certainly not likely to be as objective as someone from the outside. That's why people hire coaches or join job support groups. They do not want to wear out their families. Instead, family and friends may be better at providing some of the personally stabilizing functions like cheerleading, unconditional love, and soul nurturing. Even within these types of support, the friend who can best challenge you and give you realistic feedback may not be the one who is strongest at providing unconditional love.

Many people will find holes in their network when it comes to the different types of help they need. Perhaps your network was fine when things were going well. However, when the chips are down, the people you spent the most time with may not, for whatever reason, be able to help you get through the abyss of career change. If this describes you, know that you're certainly not alone.

Sometimes, due to circumstances, we may have surrounded ourselves with people unable to be useful to others. Consider that a lesson for yourself and make a plan to start finding some new friends.

Step Three: Convey and Negotiate Your Needs

This is the action step, and you need to take action for things to happen. Don't just expect people to intuit what you want and then feel resentful because they haven't done what you were thinking. The following are pointers on conveying needs and negotiating with others.

Educate and Re-educate

Janice told her mother she needed to take time to figure out what was best. She also educated her on the stages she was confronting in the transition. For the first week, Janice had to tell her Mom all of this a number of times. Finally her mother understood, and instead of finding Janice a job, one of her new goals included educating all her own friends on Janice's Neutral Zone and what that entailed.

It's important to educate the people around you on what career change is about for you. It's easy for others to be unhelpful to us without really understanding what they are doing. You may even show them parts of this chapter to give them a clear picture of what you need.

Most people can be fairly self-absorbed and your network is probably like that too. Don't think that just because you filled in key people on what you are going through, they will necessarily remember. I teach people the assertiveness technique called "a broken record." Smile, tell people nicely where you are at and what you need, and recognize that once may not be enough. Patiently repeat. Smile. And repeat.

Make Clear Requests

The best way to get the help you need is to be clear with others. For example, "Here's what I would find helpful from my friends during this time, if you can." Or, "Here's how you could help me."

Point Out the Elephant

Many people will want to help you but won't know what to do. They can start to avoid you unless you tell them what you'd like or that you're okay without their help for now. Especially after being laid off or fired, you need to deal with the issue head on: "As you may know, I left my company. It is difficult but I want you to know I am doing okay. The best way my friends like you can help is just to keep up our friendship now. Don't worry. If I need anything in the process of moving ahead, I'll ask you." Surfacing the issue can make the relationship easier for both people.

Create Exchanges

It's easy to see yourself as a victim in job transition. Get that behind you and make yourself useful to those you are relying upon. Think about their worlds. What do they need? What would make life easier for them?

Sometimes this exchange is explicit. "Look, if I can use your computer today, I'll make dinner for you." Or, "Help me think through this strategy, and I'll have my own mind free to help you plan your next ad campaign." Other times it is less clear what the exchange is, aside from you making progress and your friends having the pleasure of being instrumental in it. Even so, try to figure out how you can help the person you want help from. Go down the list of helpful actions above and consider what you can give back.

Expand Your Inner Circle

It might be important for you to build your network during your transition. Those who have gone through a change are often very helpful in providing kinship, listening, advice, a sounding board, and practical help with career transition roles. Kindred spirits these days are easier to find, since there are a number of public support groups, classes, and seminars on career change. If all else fails, go to the bookstore or library; you'll find people working on their searches. This could be a rare opportunity to establish relationships you'll enjoy for the rest of your life.

Help Others First

I'm a firm believer in the adage "What goes around, comes around." Helping someone else is often the first place to start. Don't assume the person you are helping will be the one who helps you. Just being helpful is a way of beginning to negotiate your needs.

Step Four: Manage Your Support Network

Sound strange? If you want people to help, you need to take on an ongoing management role. The following sections give some ideas on how to do this.

Express Appreciation

It's easy to take things for granted. Give praise and tell people what you like about what they have done. Acknowledge any actions that even look like something helpful. Often people do things for us half way or later than we expected. Be gracious and thank them for all of it. You'll get what you focus on with others.

Rotate Your Requests

Don't rely on one person for the same thing over and over. Everyone, even your truest and bluest friends, will wear out. Give them a break and spread your needs out over a number of people if you can. Be disciplined and force yourself to do this.

Keep People Posted

Sometimes people complain to me, "Diane, I sat down with so-and-so and gave her a number of suggestions. That was weeks ago and I have no idea what ever happened after that!" Or, "I couldn't believe that so-and-so was interested in working at company X and didn't even try to see if I could help him out! Why didn't he include me in things?"

Maybe you don't want to bother someone who helped you early on and so you decide not to contact her further. This is a mistake. Most people will wonder how you are. Especially if there is nothing you need from them right now, check in with people at reasonable intervals to keep them invested in your progress. Take it as a responsibility to keep in touch with people who have helped you. If you've dropped out of touch with someone for more than a month, send a short email to say hi and give an update.

Career transition is an interpersonal project. You cannot do this alone and it's silly to try. Take time to develop a language for what you really want from others, recognizing that needs may change over time. Objectively consider the strengths of your current inner circle of friends and family. Convey and negotiate for what you need and want. Recognize that many people will need to expand their relationship roles, learn new behaviors in their current relationships, and develop new connections to successfully move through a career transition. Be prepared to be clear about what you'd like and help others out as a means of helping yourself. Mastering this area of your life will help you in your next career, regardless of what it is, and in your life overall. Helping people to help you is a lesson with lifelong value.

WRITING REFLECTION EXERCISES

1. How satisfied are you with the help your friends and family give you?

2. What are the key strengths of your network of support?

3. What type of help do you most need now? Create a profile of the kind of help you need. What kind of helpers would you like more of in your support net?

4. How helpful are you to others? What are you currently best at doing? With whom?

5. How comfortable are you at conveying your needs to others?

6. What is your primary method for negotiating your needs?

7. What is the most important thing you learned from this chapter?

8. What will you do next as a result of reading this chapter?

CHAPTER TEN

LESSONS AND REFLECTIONS

Here's the most valuable lesson I've learned in my transition: I am smarter if I let the experience of others in the same place intertwine with my life. I've learned that there is nothing more powerful for me than connecting with others, both for the similarities in our experience and the differences we bring. I welcome those who have been in a completely different career to share their experience. The perspectives on our humanity are wonderful. We all are looking to bring something to this world that in the meantime will please us too. The value for me is being a part of the story.

Gretchen, forty-two, regional account manager in advertising working on a job and career change, salary high $40s

Often our best learning does not come from formal classes or even books we've read. It's from our life experiences. Hopefully you've seen by now that in the middle of puzzling and difficult times, it is often transforming to ask: *What is my lesson here? What have I learned so far?* Insisting there is a lesson gives you a sense of control and power to make your life more meaningful. Instead of being bitter and resentful, your experience in career transition can make you wiser and more realistic, and yet still allow you to dream bigger.

However, in the midst of our own transitions, it can be hard to figure out what the real lessons are. In this final chapter I will share with you some of the lessons others have found as well as my personal reflections on career change today.

LESSONS LEARNED

Some of these lessons are reminders of one we learned earlier. Some are novel, and the book would be incomplete without them. Some are fine points and some are very weighty; all are worth considering.

Change Happens and You Can Manage It

Buddhists call it impermanence; the constant is that things will change. You can learn to find your power while in the midst of change.

> I learned that nothing is forever. Life is about change. I can't stick my head in the sand, since change will happen anyway. I will strive to be all I can be and acquire as many skills as I can. My skills and accomplishments give power, which leads ultimately to knowing that employers need me and want me, and I have choices.
>
> Abe, mid-forties, currently an accountant and a part-time college teacher, describing his job change that transpired during the last year, salary mid $50s

> Life goes on. I've lost my brother—he died—and I eventually found I can still be happy and positive and he stays with me, in my heart. And the most basic thing is to be a good person, in small and big ways. That's how I manage change.
>
> Rosalie, early forties, assistant editor for a small newspaper, looking for a new position

Job Loss Can Happen at Any Age

In our culture now it is a brutal reality that you can always be involuntarily terminated, no matter who you are. So you must stay current, marketable, and connected with others in your profession outside of your organization.

> The most unexpected parts of this transition are: 1) the company was sold; 2) the two oldest employees were let go—including me. Everyone was very pleased with the training

material I'd just developed. This was the job to see me into retirement. I never would have predicted this.

Nathan, mid-forties, clinical psychologist who worked in health care, laid off from position six months ago, salary $50,000

Your Job May Not Fit You for Life

Many of us expect to find that *one* perfect job that will suit us forever. It sounds great, but we continue to grow and change, and the world around us does too.

Outgrowing this job may be a natural development. There is nothing wrong with me because I'm dissatisfied at work. It's a natural progression of growth. Answers can be found; they are there if I just listen to them and take action. It's part of the human condition; I'm not alone in this.

Katrine, forty-three, college instructor who has been working on a career change off and on for four years, salary mid $30s

It's Okay

After you've gone through layers of uncertainty about what you want and how to get it, you may come to a point of peace. Being able to develop a sense of trust in the transition process is a blessing. It makes the process go easier and better.

I know my situation can be frustrating, but it's okay, because I'm working on it. I know that the time it's taking is just too long, but it's okay. I know how frustrating, how slow, how imperfect the whole process is, but it will be okay. I'm learning about myself—things I've never thought of before—and it's empowering. So, no matter how bad it gets, it's okay.

Philip, thirty, chief engineer in radio broadcasting, seeking a career or job change for about one year, salary $50,000

Transition Involves Many Steps

There are many different steps to make in changing career direction. Most people do not understand this. It can be especially surprising when the change was their own idea.

This large transition is made of smaller ones. I didn't expect that. I thought there would be a more abrupt break from one situation and the start of a new one.

Gwyneth, professor and director for a major university, fifty-six years old, salary $55,000, currently navigating a shift in career

Patience Empowers

This is a thread that weaves throughout the book. Most people struggle with having patience. When you understand that you need to be patient and work with your transition, you can feel empowered.

Patience is a word I couldn't comprehend a few months ago. I have had little patience. Now I have much more, but I still need to work on being patient, take a day at a time. Not so easy when I usually have been a few days or years ahead instead of in the present. Other valuable things:
- spend money wisely
- get arrangements with employers in writing

Rose, mid-fifties, former teacher and small business owner who is currently trying to decide what she really wants to do

More Education Can Be a Partial Answer

Education itself is often not the whole answer to securing a new or better job, especially for mid-life career changers. Additional training is a big investment of time and energy for busy adults and it sometimes isn't worth that cost.

Most unexpected was how difficult it would be to break into a new field where I thought I could create some visibility by completing a prestigious master's program. I wasn't feeling confident about the knowledge that was jam-packed into my head in ten-week quarters. There was no time to digest the information since I was also working while taking classes. Slowly the knowledge has begun to have more form and function, but I fear taking something less than I'm truly qualified for. I also feel that a large chasm has to be crossed before real connections to a job will be made. Contacts for jobs haven't been forthcoming. No one has been as helpful as I had hoped. I'll claw my way in if necessary.

Amy, early thirties, recent MBA, looking for a new position longer than she expected—six months

To increase skills and confidence for a successful career change, many also do volunteer work or become active in associations.

Networking Is Essential

Most people don't think about having a network until they need one. Not having a job forces you to build relationships to help you find the next right opportunity. Most people do not enjoy networking initially since they are unsure what others can do for them. Making contacts takes practice. People often expect too much or too little from it. Frank is someone who came to use networking well and might have some guidance for you.

Networking works. People do care, if you take care of yourself through nutrition, fitness, spirituality, and fun. By being connected and involved with the world you are able to see yourself through other people and that will lead to insights. Start networking or informational interviewing. Call each person that you want to meet with and ask them for twenty to thirty minutes of their time to sit down and talk in the next two to three weeks. It works! Then when meeting with them, ask them for three names to contact. Getting out there and talking to people gets one in touch with the true pulse of the workplace. Listen, listen, listen.

Frank, late thirties, unemployed six months after working as a retail floor manager, looking for a new position for three months

You Can Realize What's Important to You

During your transition, you can learn what you'll need from your next job. After your job is over, it is often easier to determine what you valued most about it.

I learned how much I value working with others and having a sense of belonging to a group and being valued for my contribution. Although I have enjoyed the freedom of working independently, it somehow doesn't match the regular income and camaraderie that develops along with the energy and inspiration that I get from other people when I work for a company.

Gena, late forties, independent consultant and career changer, has been looking for a new position longer than she expected—a year and a half

Your Thinking Doesn't Have to Cripple Your Progress

Your thinking and beliefs, especially about yourself, can cripple you in transition even more than they did at work. If you are open to examining them, the dysfunctional patterns of your thinking can become clearer to you. You also have a rare opportunity to change them.

I knew that having left the firm I had a lot of negative emotions built up that I needed to address. However, I had no idea that I would uncover—with my therapist's help—so many thinking paradigms that were making my life miserable and anxious. We've discovered about a dozen paradigms so far. Things including "not worthy without a real job," "not good enough if I don't have a lot of friends," looking at situations with black instead of rose colored glasses.

212

Understanding these thinking paradigms made me feel much better and be more present in most situations. I am more comfortable with myself. I also did not expect that the search would take this long, but maybe I'll learn something else in the remaining time.

Jeff, early forties, formerly director of marketing for mid-sized firm, salary $60,000

The more positive I am, the better the outcome of anything I am working on. Even if it does not produce the final desired result, it moves me further through the process than I would have been if I were negative. When I focus on negative things they come in plentiful abundance, which in turn only makes me more negative. Whatever I have focused on in a positive way, I have gotten in some form.

Daniel, mid-twenties, account representative for a temporary agency, salary $30,000, looking for job and career change for the last nine months

You Must Confront Your Feelings

Buried fear and anger often make themselves known when we try to make a transition. They exhibit the Ping-Pong Ball Effect that I mentioned earlier, surfacing as soon as we are not actively trying to push them down. Digging deep and confronting these emotions is often important to do before you can move on.

My greatest lesson is to look squarely at my fear of not being good enough at work. Face your greatest fear, warrior woman. On the other side of the fence is the green pasture— the sun shines, opportunity knocks. I walk deliberately and humbly. I'm in control. It's okay, whatever the outcome may be. I welcome the change, yet still resist it. I dig into the catacombs of my life. I can face this fear and become stronger.

Francis, early forties, currently a director of accounting in the financial services industry, salary $90,000

As she poetically confronts her fear, Francis can put it to rest. Freedom!

> The best advice I could give someone is to talk, complain, cry, write, and express yourself as much as you can. Bring your anger to the surface, recognize it, and get it out. Releasing negative feelings in a safe environment has helped me stay calmer in an interview situation, where showing strong emotions is unacceptable.
>
> Kristen, late thirties, testing coordinator in a small consulting firm

Hindsight Can Provide Insight

In transition, especially if you have left your job, you may be able to see yourself more clearly. After you leave a work situation completely, you may be able to get a better view of your limitations; this is good but not always comfortable. Here's an example of a limitation many have—the inability to say no.

> Looking back I can see that many times at work I would just tell people what they wanted to hear—your order will be ready when you need it and adding extra items to it will be no problem. I wanted them to like me and just have everyone think everything was okay. Then I would spend my time and sometimes money making things work for them. I couldn't say no and got very worn out. I ended up getting behind in my work, especially since I felt no one else could do what I did or do it as well. What I learned in this was how much I needed to change. My lesson was that I need to be realistic and tell others the truth even if it's hard to say. It was really just an unnecessary pattern.
>
> Jamie, fifty-one, sales manager for a pharmaceutical company, terminated from his position seven months ago, salary $110,000

Appreciate Work When It Works

Once you've been in a job you don't like, you can more easily appreciate work situations that are better for you. The one you hated can make your wiser about what you have when you finally find that great job.

> The most valuable thing I have learned so far is to not take job satisfaction for granted. If you like what you're doing, enjoy it while it lasts.
>
> Kristen, late thirties, testing coordinator in a small consulting firm

You Are More Valuable than You Might Think

Very few of the people I see in coaching have received useful feedback in their work life. Think about it—usually the best things you think *about* other people, you probably would not say *to* them, much less the worst. Performance reviews rarely present a clear picture of the broad scope of your skills and strengths. At best, they are focused only on your job. We often say the most appreciative things about other people at their funerals.

> It's so valuable to me to have people around me who think very highly of me. They have given me advice—said the difficult things. They have pointed out my skills and shown me they are willing to support me with a reference or a referral.
>
> Maggie, mid-fifties, laid off one month ago from her position of six years as a communications specialist, seeking a career change

Commitment Matters

We would all like to have changes made without having to stick out our necks and invest the time and energy. While there can be some magic, coincidence, and synchronicity to developing your career, the commitment of your energy is essential.

> I know now that I need to commit to making a change in my life, not just wishing for it to happen; that it is possible to have a fulfilling career and, as result, a more fulfilling life; that

there are so many options out there; and that I need to invest the time in myself and my future to find the right one(s).

Jacob, mid-thirties, left his position as a technical writer for a software company three months ago for a career change

Reading Can Help Immensely

There are countless career books out there now, and it might be hard to figure out what else to read. Here are a couple of key books that have worked for others.

The most basic "must do" is to read the *What Color Is Your Parachute?* book. It's a good foundation for any transition. If you are thinking about a transition, read it. If you have already started your transition, read it as soon as possible. Whatever route you take, this is the best starting point to get all your affairs in order. Even if you are not any clearer about what you want to do after reading it, your starting block is in place.

Daniel, mid-twenties, account representative for a temporary agency, salary $30,000, looking for job and career change for the last nine months

Anyone anticipating a transition should read Carol Kleiman's column in the *Chicago Tribune* (online and syndicated).

Jan, early forties, employed floral assistant looking to make a career change

Your Own Reactions May Surprise You

Even when changes are our choice and are positive events, you can still expect an array of emotional responses, including anger and depression. Your own frustration with your feelings can also intensify and prolong them.

My tendency toward the dramatic—my ability to catastrophize—was unexpected. I've only been in Chicago for two months; been looking for a job while also planning a wedding, temping, and getting settled here. Not very focused. Don't think that anyone would expect me to have a job yet or be decided on a direction after just finishing school, yet I feel scared that I don't have a job. I worry that I'll never find the right thing. It's not logical, doesn't follow, and I'm sure it isn't true, yet I continue to struggle with thinking about this in dramatic, catastrophizing terms. Very unlike me, very unexpected.

Jennifer, twenty-five, completed graduate school two months ago

By looking at your life for lessons, you can see your story and be the hero of your life, rather than a victim. In your transition, keep your learning attitude; take the time regularly to write out what you are learning. Keep a notebook with you. Whether your insights are large or small, you can use them to experience and create the work and life you want most.

REFLECTIONS

When I started to think about this book, I wanted to help people capitalize on the opportunity that transition can bring. It seemed that many people felt alone and confused and needed guidance on how to handle their emotional underpinnings—the essentials that could sabotage them or make them very successful.

There were a number of things I did not expect—for example, that the emotional texture of my own experience would be either matched or foreshadowed by many of the topics I had committed to write about. I had no idea that all the fear, ambiguity, interminable frustration, and painful rejection that my clients experience in navigating career changes would become part of my own life. I wrote about rejection, I got it. I wrote about ambiguity, it surrounded me. I wrote about deep frustration and anger, and they became a part of my life for numerous reasons. And then when I wrote about intuition, I realized that it was a gift to be able to write at times in such an effortless and euphoric flow. I felt more alive and present than I have ever felt in my entire life. I also didn't expect to find such a fine home for this book with people who could truly love it and help craft its messages. Nor did I expect the grace and tenacity displayed by my husband, who worked diligently on this project with me while taking care of many other parts of our life.

This is a time when many people have struggled a great deal and lost dreams, jobs, financial security and even more. My personal experiences and those of my clients—in the midst of a challenging and changing world—have brought me additional insights I'd like to share in closing.

On Technology and Illusion

I've seen more and more that in a career transition, computer technology and the Internet can be a blessing or a curse depending on how you use them. In a world of instant messages and the ability to send out résumés with the click of a mouse, people develop illusions about how productive they are. It's addictive to sit and go through Internet postings and your email. You feel like you're doing something. In reality, unless you're in computer science, you probably won't find a job on the Internet. Not only that, because of the glut of responses companies get, you are unlikely to hear back from anyone after emailing your carefully crafted résumé. It's easy to feel depressed by that and many people do. Don't spend your time doing things that make you depressed because they are unproductive.

And yet cyberspace offers tremendous utility for navigating change. The Internet is great for researching companies, understanding what's going on in the world, and getting the daily news. It's an excellent way to stay connected to the world when you don't have a job. And you should certainly consider job postings as part of a broader job search strategy. However, don't let cyberspace become your mirage and waste your time. Be conscious of how and why you are using the web and then use it to your best advantage. Make powerful choices.

On Redwoods and Power

I've been haunted by the sight of the redwoods I saw this summer, described in chapter seven. These magnificent beauties weather the elements, grow to amazing proportions, and live for many years. They are anchored by roots that are shallow but vastly wide and that knit them firmly together. Very recently, the reason for my fascination came to me. In some ways, I think we're similar to the redwood trees. We too can grow proud, strong, and tall from the webbing we make, the kind of interconnections that join us with others. So as you proceed, if you feel lost and alone, try reaching out to others, ask for their help, and don't be afraid to help others too. Since we are all interconnected, your efforts will come back to you.

On Dreams, Emotional Employment, and Daily Life

It's important to have a dream or vision of your perfect career or life. You often do get what you focus on, whether it's your hope or your fear. Yet especially in a tough economy, you won't always get what you expect or even deserve.

If dreams don't turn out the way we expect, we need to accept our reactions, to learn from them, and to dream again. Living a life driven by your deepest purpose and passion is its own reward. And maybe what really matters more than achieving all your dreams is being able to truly show up—to be present—for your own life, whatever that is.

Self-knowledge is the foundation of job satisfaction and fulfillment. Emotional employment—the marriage of your talents and work—is when you can truly be yourself on the job and therefore can give it your strongest commitment. As we all stumble our way through a changing world of work, we may need other skills to find emotional employment. Most importantly you need to love what you can about what you have right now and build a life that is rich enough to support you while you move toward your dreams.

Maybe your daily work matches your soul's desires some days, and other days it doesn't. And on those days when it doesn't, it becomes your teacher. My wish for you is that you can be truly

219

present for your lessons and let life be your teacher. You're not alone in this—we're all learning together.

ACKNOWLEDGEMENTS

Writing a book is a lot like making a career transition; it takes a village and has its own journey. A number of very special people helped directly and indirectly to bring this to fruition.

My first recognition goes to those whose quotes and stories appear throughout the book. Most of the quotes are from people who attended a series of writing workshops I conducted during 2000-2002. Their writings were sometimes edited or shaped to develop specific points. Some quotes and all the stories are actually composites of people I have known through my life and practice. To protect privacy, all names and specifically identifying information have been changed. Nonetheless, I think you can feel the spirit, struggles, and courage of many people in these pages. I thank you all.

Early on, three people helped me get this project off the ground. Al Gustafson from the Crossroads Center intuitively understood the project from my first thoughts on it and also served as a rather consistent "touch point" and supporter throughout the later phases of the writing and production. Tom Murray, as the executive director of the Career Transitions Center of Chicago, sponsored the recruitment of many of the participants. Lynn Staudacher, a very talented writing teacher, helped me conduct the first writing workshops.

At the core of my work and world is now and has been my large, wonderful family. I am forever grateful to my parents, Laura and James Grimard, Sr.; my brothers, James, Jr., Tom, Joe, Richard and Daniel Grimard; my sisters, Mary Brunais and Sharon Calkins and their families. My "other" self-created family, best and good friends, listened for hours to my hopes and dreams for this book and its messages: Laura Wimbish-Vanderbeck, Teresa Spano Bradley, Lani

Granum, Madelyn Iglar, Elizabeth (Beth) Shannon, Elene Cafasso, Katherine (K) Foran and Liz Peterson.

My business and life strategy group of three years is the best anyone could ever imagine. This includes my enthusiastic and faithful supporter Linda Liang and the guys-Craig Kanter, Uri Heller, and George Savarese. Their dreams for my life are always larger than mine. Two other key people are Carol Kleiman, best-selling author and syndicated newspaper columnist for the *Chicago Tribune*, who has been a role model and inspiration and Richard Bolles, author of *What Color Is Your Parachute?*, who has been a wonderful friend, teacher, and inspiration. Dick, I'm glad to still have your presence in my life and everyone else's!

Bob and Harolyn Thompson provided technical advice as well emotional support for the conception, writing, and publishing of this book. Bob is the author of over thirty books in the wine and food area. Over a period of years and many wonderful dinners together, Bob consistently told my husband Gary and me that he knew I would write a book someday. His vision and confidence helped me shape mine. His accomplishments and high-integrity work inspire me greatly.

I've had the honor of having many talented teachers, editors, and colleagues. Across the years, patient teachers have influenced my skills-including Robert Slaney, Joseph Stokes, Paul Sackett, Carol North, S.L. Wisenberg, and Nina Barrett. Each of these people taught very important things. I also am very grateful to other writers, editors, and friends who helped me to find, remember, and develop my own writing voice and navigate the publishing process: Stefania Aulucino, Claudia Banks, Anita Brick, Jack Thompson, Rochelle Kopp, Ellie Workman, Laurie Kahn, Angela Popolla, Marcia Pradzinski, Diane Fisher, Arlene Hirsch, Barbara Grauer, Polly Jensen, Randi Killian, John Grobe, and Sheila Seclearr. Other editorial input and wise coaching along the way came from K. Foran, Peg Hendershot, and Leah Yarrow. Sandi Wisenberg reviewed almost every single word of the first draft of this book-although I'll take any blame. Connie Shaw, my publisher, skillfully polished this work with uncommon diligence to retaining its own voice.

My thanks for Sheree Bykofsky and Megan Buckley for loving and having faith in this project long before anyone else in the publishing world did. Joel Saltzman, writer and comedian, provided inspiration for my book with his own-especially *Always Kiss Me Goodnight.* His smart, warm, and witty correspondence at key points in the process kept me going.

As a writer, it's been so valuable to know people who day-to-day remain persistently optimistic, interested, and even excited about your progress long after you've decided you'll never be finished (ever). My team members from the Chicagoland Chamber of Commerce Workplace Excellence Committee were the best, especially Bill Holland, PhD; Isis Garcia; Gary Cohen; John Roback; Jody Coveny; Coleman Connelly; Bill Hensky; and Mary Clark. So were folks from my health club-especially staff members Shelley Heard and Eric Greiner-and my Tae Kwon Do buddies Richard Reichstein, Dr. Milli Bahn, Robert Shearn, Mark Friedland, Paul, and Julius Ranses.

Similarly, the staff at my "base camp," Caribou Coffee in Oak Park, Illinois, including Juan Gutierrez, the manager, was great. I will always appreciate their kindness and ability to take some level of joy in my presence there for days and months on end, their excitement as the project "brewed" along, and all the good coffee that made it happen. I thank the many supportive kindred spirits I met there including Gordon Brumwell, Jessie Faulk, and the studious, nice, and overworked medical students who also spent days on end at "The Bou." I also had the fortune of finding other homes in great coffee places. I'm especially grateful to the staff at Starbucks in Oak Park and in Chicago at Hubbard and Franklin for their kindness and support.

Words can't describe my feelings for Gary Wilson, my partner, business manager, wrangler, agent, editor, and spouse extraordinaire. He left his full-time job to work in our company so he could join me in bringing this together. Gary has a rare combination of fine intelligence, uncompromising objectivity, and a great heart.

I am grateful to other special people in our lives who have provided invaluable help and support in different ways: Colleen May, The Venerable Dr. Boonshoo Sriburin, Donna Sandberg, Mike Iglar, Donna St. Aubin, Manny Sanchez, Diane Huntley, Julius Ranses, Harry McBride, Pati Soto, and Phyllis Joelson.

To my many other friends and fellows committed to sane, honest, and inspired relationships to work, money, and life, thank you for sharing your experience, strength, and hope, and for continually inspiring me.

Last, and certainly not least, thank you, thank you to the team at Sentient Publications including Nick Cummings, Joe Braidish, Fred Taylor, Parm Dhillon, and especially publisher Connie Shaw. Together, your belief in this book has anchored my life. Your love and care in producing it has never failed to amaze me. Connie, you trusted your own intuition that my book might help others and shepherded me, a first time author, through its creation with both kindness and grace. My deepest and most sincere gratitude.

NOTES

Introduction

3   "Further, research shows . . ." U.S. Department of Labor Statistics. 2002.

3   "Sigmund Freud said that mentally healthy people . . ." Freud, Sigmund. *The Psychopathology of Everyday Life.* Penguin Classics, 2003.

Chapter One. Get Smart About What's Happening

13   "Some of the stages of grieving Dr. Elizabeth Kubler-Ross identified . . ." Kubler-Ross, Elizabeth. *On Death and Dying.* Scribner, 1997.

20   "In working with my clients, I have found the writings of William Bridges . . ." Bridges, William. *Transitions: Making Sense of Life's Changes.* Perseus Publishing, 1980.

      This book is a classic; it paints a picture of the psychological architecture of transition. Some people who have read it, say it changed their life. That's why I felt was essential to include Bridges' framework in Back in Control.

Chapter Two. Know Your Own Story

32   "Writing your story . . ." Pennebaker, James W. *Opening Up: The Healing Power of Expressing Emotions.* Guildford Press, 1997.

This book is a compilation of Pennebaker's research on the effect of writing your feelings down on paper. Very compelling.

Chapter Three. Recognize Key Challenges and Personal Barriers

55   "One framework useful for understanding . . ."

The ideas on the Safe-Keeping and Experimental Selves are used with permission. This framework was part of a fifteen-day training program called Spirituality and Career Development given by Richard Bolles, author of What Color Is Your Parachute? I participated in this program in August, 1991.

Chapter Four. Tap into the Power of Style

80   "While there are a number of different frameworks . . ." *Facilitator Manual for DiSC.* Minneapolis, Minnesota: Inscape Publishing, 2003.

94   "Simply put: You build relationships . . ."

This framework, which relates elements of trust to DiSC dimensions, comes is adapted from a series of presentations given by Keith Ayers at the Inscape Publishing Annual Business Conferences in 2000-2003.

Chapter Five. Condition Your Mind for Success

113 "As the Buddhist teachers say . . ." Smith, Jean. *Breath Sweeps Mind: A First Guide to Meditation Practice.* New York: Berkeley Publishing Group, 1998.

This book is a collection of writings from celebrated meditation teachers including the Buddha, Thich Nhat Hanh, and Sylvia Boorstein. The articles are short and easy to digest. They capture the important principles behind the art.

117 "Psychologist Martin Seligman says . . ." Seligman, Martin, and others. *Conditioned Helpless: A Theory for the Age of Personal Control.* Oxford University Press, 1995.

119 "Millions of people . . ." *Alcoholics Anonymous.* New York: Alcoholics Anonymous World Services, 1939.

This presents the basic twelve-step spiritual program for recovering from compulsive behavior. It focuses on alcoholism but the handbook has been used for other self-destructive behaviors such as over-eating, overspending, and drug addiction.

Chapter Six. Let Your Emotions Be Your Strength

131 "I call this the Ping-Pong Ball Effect . . ." Mother's Wisdom. My mother first gave me the analogy of emotions being like a ping pong ball in a glass of water. From this, I coined the term Ping-Pong Ball Effect.

141 "I recommend that people read Julia Cameron's . . ." Cameron, Julia. *The Artist's Way: A Spiritual Path to Higher Creativity.* G.P. Putnam's Sons, 1992.

145 "Every challenge we face . . ." My thoughts in this section have been deeply influenced by Marianne Williamson's book *Return to Love: Reflections on the Principles of a Course in Miracles.* New York: HarperPerrennial, 1992.

Chapter Seven. Cultivate Intuitive Guidance

157 "I attended a workshop . . ." Childre, Doc, and Bruce Cryer, Bruce. *From Chaos to Coherence (the power to change performance).* Boulder Creek, California: Planetary, 2000.

This book summarizes research of the HeartMath™ Foundation.

163 "Then one summer . . ." *The Tall Trees: Portraits of California's Redwood Parks, Preserves and Visitor Attractions.* Fortuna, California: FVN Corporation, 2001.

This is an excellent guidebook I came across on the redwoods while visiting that area.

169 "The Dalai Lama has said . . ." His Holiness The Dalai Lama. *An Open Heart: Practicing Compassion in Everyday Life.* Boston: Little Brown, and Company, 2001.

170 "The key is . . ." Chan, Achaan, and others. *Still Forest Pool: The Insight Meditation of Achaan Chan.* Theosophical Publishing House, 1985.

RESOURCES

I n addition to the books I have listed in the Notes section, these are some of my favorite resources for managing career transition and increasing emotional employment. Any of the following books and CDs can be easily accessed through our website at *www.Back-In-Control.com*. Many of these resources could fit into more than one category and sometimes the author has other books you many want to consider, which I'll describe.

CAREER RESOURCES

Self Assessment

Bolles, Richard N. *What Color Is Your Parachute? A Practical Manual for Job-Hunters and Career-Changers.* Berkeley, CA: Ten Speed Press, 2004.

Published every year since 1972; always a best-seller. The thrust of Bolles' work is to give a practical framework to navigate the job search process and up-to-the-minute tips for finding the ideal career. This book is wonderful but can appear a little overwhelming. My favorite parts are the skills exercises, especially the seven stories and the Flower Exercise which are usually in Appendix A. Bolles rigorously updates this book annually and does all the writing, editing, and even the layout himself.

Boldt, Laurence G. *Zen and the Art of Making a Living: A Practical Guide to Creative Career Design.* Compass, 1999.

Full of rich ideas and strategies, *Zen* has more than 120 work-sheets and 500 inspirational quotes. Boldt's intent is to cultivate self-awareness and spirit for everyday life and work and to use that to find meaningful work. This is a wonderful book for philosophers, seekers, and readers looking to put soul into their work. *Zen* covers a comprehensive range of career topics such as selecting and securing the work, entrepreneurship, and even starting a foundation.

Helfand, David, Ph.D. *Career Change: Everything You Need to Know to Meet New Challenges and Take Control of Your Career.* McGraw Hill, 1995.

A bible and guide for career changers covering practical steps and important realities such as dealing with a tight job market, balancing time and money in career investments, and researching companies. Gives emphasis to special needs groups including women, minorities, over fifty, disabled, and ex-military.

Lore, Nicholas. *The Pathfinder: How to Choose or Change Your Career for a Lifetime of Satisfaction and Success.* New York: Simon & Schuster, 1998.

Based on work of the award-winning career counseling network Rockport Institute, this comprehensive book guides readers from beginning to end in choosing or changing careers. It will help you tackle resume writing and contains more than one hundred self-tests and diagnostic tools to help assess values, goals, and strengths.

Finding Passion and Meaning in Work and Life

Sher, Barbara. *I Could Do Anything If I Only Knew What It Was: How to Discover What You Really Want and How to Get It.* DTP, 1995.

Barbara Sher is a great inspiration to all. This book is a classic and she has written others since, including *Wishcraft.* It's designed to help you find your passion and get on with your life.

Bronson, Po. *What Should I Do With My Life? The True Story of People Who Answered the Ultimate Question.* New York: Random House, 2002.

Journalist Po Bronson traveled the country in search of answers, asking others: *How do you find purpose and passion in your life and work? When do you know you have it?* His book is a collection of fifty-five stories from people of many walks of life. With these great stories Bronson raises and explores many issues related to work and life meaning. His recent paperback updates and expands the original stories.

Leider, Richard J. and Shapiro, David A. *Repacking Your Bags: Lighten Your Load for the Rest of Your Life.* Second Edition. San Francisco: Berrett-Koehler, 2002.

This international bestseller helps you understand what makes you happy and how to create that in three key areas of life-work, relationships, and place or home. *Repacking* is filled with stories, personal examples, and exercises to help you evaluate the burdens you are carrying and to distill out what's important. It's a map for purposeful living.

Searching For the Job

www.JobHuntersBible.com

This is an excellent one-stop career site constructed to be a supplement to Bolles' *What Color Is Your Parachute?* It has two parts: The Net Guide to direct you to key career resource sites on the Internet for things such as easy research and free testing and the Parachute Library-a growing collection of articles written by Bolles and close colleagues on job search.

Kleiman, Carol. *Winning the Job Game: New Rules for Finding and Keeping the Job You Want.* Hoboken, New Jersey: John Wiley & Sons, 2002.

An excellent book on how to find and keep a job in the new world of work. Written in a supportive and humorous tone, Kleiman's topics include how to negotiate a salary, prepare for an interview and performance review, and advance your career through continuing your education. Two of the ten chapters present summaries of the fastest growing careers, their salaries, and training needed.

Interviewing and Writing Resumes and Cover Letters

Enelow, Wendy S. *Best Keywords for Resumes, Cover Letters, and Interviews: Powerful Communications Tools for Success.* Manassas Park, VA: Impact Publications, 2003.

_____. *Key Words to Nail Your Job Interview: What to Say to Win Your Dream Job.* Manassas Park, VA: Impact Publications, 2004.

_____. *Best Resumes for People Without a Four-Year Degree.* Manassas Park, VA: Impact Publications, 2004.

_____. *Best Resumes For $100,000+ Jobs.* Manassas Park, VA: Impact Publications, 2002.
Wendy S. Enelow has authored a number of excellent books on how to write resumes and cover letters and master the interview. Search through more of her books for ones to fit your specific needs.

WRITING YOUR STORY

Anderson, Nancy. *Work With Passion.* Novato, CA: New World Library, 1996.
This book helps people take "Know Your Own Story" a step further. The main thrust of her book is a method for writing an autobiography of your life. This can be a very powerful tool in making a career change. I have met people I felt just needed to write out their life story in some detail before they could move on; this book helps them.

TAPPING INTO THE POWER OF YOUR BEHAVIORAL STYLE

If you are interested in learning more about your DiSC behavioral style, through using a tool that assesses your style and gives you a customized report, go to our website: *www.Back-In-Control.com.* Click: Online tools.

MENTAL CONDITIONING

Grabhorn, Lynn. *Excuse Me Your Life Is Waiting: The Astonishing Power of Feelings.* Charlottesville, Virginia: Hampton Roads Publishing Company, 2000.

I love this book. Grabhorn has a great writing style and presents a unique angle on the mind-feelings-and- prosperity equation. She tells us to focus first on our feelings and the rest can then come into place. An inspiring book which is also available on CD and cassette.

Joseph, Lynn, Ph.D. *The Job Loss Recovery Guide: A Proven Program for Getting Back to Work—Fast!* New Harbinger Publications, 2003.

An easy read. Dr. Joseph's approach is based on mind conditioning principles and she uses them with many aspects of job loss. The book is based on Joseph's own research which documents the positive effects.

ENHANCING EMOTIONS, LOVE, AND SPIRITUALITY

A Course in Miracles. Mill Valley, CA: Foundation for Inner Peace, Inc., 1996.

This book was first published in three volumes in 1975. It's a spiritual psychology self-study program. It's nondenominational and contains daily meditation practices to help you remove the barriers to love in your life. Studying the *Course* on your own can be powerful. Many cities have study groups and you can even find online support. Many people study the *Course* for years and claim it is a continually life-changing experience.

Loving Each Day. Free daily inspirational messages from the Movement of Spiritual Inner Awareness (MSIA).

A friend of mine, motivational speaker Sandy Karn, suggested this daily inspirational email program a few years ago and I thought, I certainly don't need another email each day. I decided to try it out and still really enjoy and look forward to it. The messages can help you see more love in your life and connect with your spirit. MSIA describes their organization *as a nondenominational, ecumenical church that teaches that each of us is divine and we can know our own divinity.* You can subscribe to this email list by visiting the MSIA website at *www.msia.org* and clicking on the Loving Each Day icon. Or send an email to: *Join-Loving-Each-Day@lists.msianet.org.*

MEDITATING AND DEVELOPING YOUR INTUITION

Beattie, Melody. *The Language of Letting Go: Daily Meditations for Codependents.* New York: Harper/Hazelton, 1991.

One of my favorite meditation books of all time on love, trust, spirituality and how to stop focusing on others and live your own life. Beattie gives you a new gem to contemplate every day.

Breathnach, Sarah. B. *The Simple Abundance Journal of Gratitude.* Warner Books, 1996.

This book gives you an excellent way to practice gratitude and helps you become more disciplined in using this powerful tool.

Choquette, Sonia. *Your Heart's Desire: Instructions for Creating the Life You Really Want.* New York: Three Rivers Press, 1997.

_____. *The Psychic Pathway: A Workbook for Reawakening the Voice of Your Soul.* Three Rivers Press, 1995.

This is a wonderful book full of tools and good stories on cultivating your intuition from America's most popular psychic-Sonia Choquette. She's written a number of books on intuition and life.

Harrison, Steven. *Getting to Where You Are: The Life of Meditation.* Boulder: Sentient Publications, 2003.

Steven Harrison, contemporary mystic, explores through a series of personal essays what meditation is and what it's not. With humor and insight, he demystifies meditation and leads readers to an appreciation of life as it is in the moment.

Smith, Jean, ed. *Breath Sweeps Mind: A First Guide to Meditation Practice.* New York: Berkeley Publishing Group, 1998.

Breath is a very good place to start if you experience with meditation is limited. It's collection of writings from celebrated meditation teachers including the Buddha, Thich Nhat Hanh, and Sylvia Boorstein. The articles capture the important principles behind the art. Each article is quite short and easy to digest.

Tolle, Eckhart. *The Power of Now.* Novato, CA: New World Library, 1999.

_____. *Practicing the Power of Now.* Novato, CA: New World Library, 2001.

_____. *Stillness Speaks.* Novato, CA: New World Library, 2003.

_____. *Entering the Now (The Power of Now Teaching Series).* Boulder: Sounds True, 2003.

Eckhart Tolle is one of my favorite teachers. His writing is so clear. You can feel his sense of presence in his books and your own sense of calm increases just from reading them. His CDs and cassettes are even better for those who prefer audio information as a portal to the present.

Simpson, Savtri. *Chakras for Starters.* Crystal Clarity Publishers, 2002.

Savitri's book and her CD by the same name will help you find and manage your heart energy and other key centers.

HeartMath, *www.heartmath.com/freeservices.html.*

Their website has a number of ongoing complementary services. These include daily memos, a weekly tip that shows you how to apply more heart at work and home, and Freeze-frame-a monthly newsletter on how to use their biofeedback software to improve your life and work.

SHAPING YOUR ENVIRONMENT FOR FOCUS AND CLARITY

Collins, Terah K. *The Western Guide to Feng Shui: Cultivating Balance, Harmony, and Prosperity in Your Environment.* Carlsbad, CA: Hay House, Inc., 1996

A readable approach to analyzing the Feng Shui of your space and making adjustments from a nationally recognized expert.

Dexter, Rosalyn. *Feng Shui: Chinese Whispers: Techniques for Transforming Life, Work and Home.* Rizzoli International Publications, 2002.

This is an exquisite gift book, oversized, and full of beautifully laid out information. The book itself illustrates the power of design and also offers numerous practical pointers to help you with home and work.

Keller, Debra. *Feng Shui,* Kansas City: Andrews McMeel Publishing, 2003.

A pocket-sized book full of great ideas.

Santo-Pierto, Nancy. *Feng Shui: Harmony by Design.* Perigree Books, 1996.

Very logical and readable text on how to assess your living environment and make the changes you need to meet your objectives.

CREATING PROSPERITY

Mundis, Jerrold. *Earn What You Deserve: How to Stop Underearning & Start Thriving.* New York: Bantam Books, 1995.

_____. *How to Get Out of Debt & Live Prosperously.* New York: Bantam Books, 1988.

If you find other books that have helped you personally and that you'd like to recommend to others, feel free to send me an email: *BackInControl1@aol.com.*

INDEX

ABOUT THE AUTHOR

Photo: Jennifer Girard

Diane Wilson, founder of Grimard Wilson Consulting, Inc., has focused more than fifteen years on issues related to the human side of work. Her background is in coaching and counseling, management training, college teaching, and organizational consulting. She has been involved in numerous projects helping individuals find personal meaning in their work as well as increase their level of competence. Diane's expertise ranges from survey research to executive coaching with special interests in career satisfaction and enhancing emotional intelligence at work.

Diane has been a contributing columnist for the *Chicago Tribune's* Working Section feature, "Insider." Her work has also appeared in the *Reader's Digest, Conscious Choice,* and in trade publications. She has been interviewed for television, radio and print periodicals including *Kiplinger's Personal Finance, Christian Science Monitor, Black Enterprise* and *Financial Times.* She is a licensed clinical professional counselor with a Master's degree in Clinical and Counseling Psychology from the University of Akron. She has continued her education in organizational dynamics, coaching, and career and executive development, including training with Richard Bolles, author of *What Color Is Your Parachute?,* and at The Center for Creative Leadership in Greensboro, North Carolina.

Sentient Publications, LLC publishes books on cultural creativity, experimental education, transformative spirituality, holistic health, new science, and ecology, approached from an integral viewpoint. Our authors are intensely interested in exploring the nature of life from fresh perspectives, addressing life's great questions, and fostering the full expression of the human potential. Sentient Publications' books arise from the spirit of inquiry and the richness of the inherent dialogue between writer and reader.

We are very interested in hearing from our readers. To direct suggestions or comments to us, or to be added to our mailing list, please contact:

SENTIENT PUBLICATIONS, LLC
1113 Spruce Street
Boulder, CO 80302
303.443.2188
contact@sentientpublications.com
www.sentientpublications.com